Etiquette
for
everyday
living

days after you have returned home. (See chapter on Correspondence.)

All of us enjoy having fellowship with those "of like precious faith," and so we enjoy entertaining our friends. But entertaining can also be an outreach. The neighbor or business acquaintance who would never attend church to hear the gospel would probably come to your home for a barbecue or for dessert and coffee some evening. Because of this his life could be changed.

Entertaining is given a new dimension if, because we invited someone to dinner, he finds Christ as his Saviour. Then he with us will eventually be a part of the great marriage supper of the Lamb spoken of in Revelation 19.

Etiquette
for
everyday
living

by
DOROTHY MARTIN

moody press
chicago

ETIQUETTE

FOR EVERYDAY LIVING

Original title:
CHRISTIAN ETIQUETTE
FOR EVERYDAY LIVING

Copyright © 1969 by
THE MOODY BIBLE INSTITUTE
OF CHICAGO

ISBN: 0-8024-2386-8

Fourth Printing, 1975

Printed in the United States of America

CONTENTS

advance what color dress the girl will be wearing so
that his choice of flowers will not clash with it. If he
hasn't done so and the color-combination is really
awful, she must accept the corsage graciously anyway,
hard as this is, and wear it. If not on her dress, then
attached to a bracelet or pinned on a small evening
bag. When flowers are worn on the dress, put them on
the way they grew—straight up. A corsage may be
brought by the man when he calls for his date, but it's
better to have it sent in advance to give the girl time to
put it on—and to get over the shock that isn't what she
hoped for.

DATES WHILE BABY-SITTING

The problem of having a date while baby-sitting can
be a tricky situation. Some employers don't mind, and
give their permission for a boyfriend to come over and
keep the baby-sitter company. Others object strenuously, particularly if it is done without their knowledge.
This is another area where a dating couple must be
careful not to give offense. After all, even having
another girl come in to help baby-sit does not necessarily mean extra protection for the children. Two
girls can get so involved in conversation that they
forget their responsibilities.

What should a girl do when a boy she would really
like to go out with calls her, but she already has a date
for that evening, or is committed to a family project,
or has a baby-sitting job she can't break? She has to
turn him down, of course, but with enough regret in
her voice that he'll know she isn't just making up an
excuse. Girls usually think they have the hard time in

INTRODUCTION

To some people etiquette is a set of rigid rules to be followed absolutely; to others it is a foolish system of outmoded conventions which are unnecessary in our casual age. Neither attitude is right. There is a commonsense approach to etiquette which lies between these two extremes.

It is this commonsense approach that puts etiquette rules in the right perspective. It *is* possible to follow the rules of correct behavior so slavishly that we leave out the most important ingredient of good manners— kindness. Too much emphasis on the outward forms of etiquette can obscure the inner spirit of courtesy. On the other hand, carelessness about etiquette gives the impression that we know and care nothing about correct behavior. Etiquette rules are elastic and often must be stretched, but not to the breaking point.

The key to this business of good manners and courteous behavior is to know the right thing to do and say, and then to do and say it naturally. Etiquette isn't a pattern of behavior which someone made up and wrote in a book, a pattern entirely different from the way we would normally act. Instead, it is a way of life which is based both on rigid traditional rules and on flexible rules of good taste and common sense.

The familiar ditty learned in childhood is still a good rule to follow:

> Politeness is to do and say
> The kindest thing in the kindest way.

Along with it must be put the ageless words of the Golden Rule: "As ye would that men should do to you, do ye also to them likewise" (Luke 6:31). It *is* better to be kind than correct if a choice must be made between them, but usually both are possible.

Then why bother with etiquette rules? Because they help us to do things "decently and in order" in our relationships with other people. Good manners are not a veneer applied over a cheap piece of wood, which may be eaten away by the least scratch or pressure. Really good manners come from within and are the gloss which enhances the bare material. They are based on consideration for others. The words of Paul in I Corinthians 13, "Charity [love] . . . is kind . . . envieth not . . . doth not behave itself unseemly . . . is not easily provoked, thinketh no evil," may be applied to good manners.

Respect for others is one of the basics of good manners, and this means that sometimes rules of etiquette must be adapted to a particular situation or culture. It means that there is no one correct way in which something must always be done, for some etiquette rules depend on where and how people live. What is acceptable one place may be rude in another. Correct behavior, then, is a commonsense application of rules of courtesy which are in keeping with the customs of the time and place.

But there are absolutes in behavior—politeness, kindness, hospitality, sympathy, consideration—which are always correct. These should be observed by the Christian even more than by others. This is because the Christian has an extra dimension in his life. He is indwelt by the Holy Spirit, and therefore his life should be characterized by "love, joy, peace, longsuf-fering, gentleness, goodness, faith, meekness, temper-ance" (Galatians 5:22-23). He is a representative of Jesus Christ and is not his own.

God says, "Ye are epistles . . . known and read of all men" (II Corinthians 3:2). It is Christ men read of in a Christian's behavior. That is why etiquette is so important for the Christian.

DOROTHY MARTIN

WEARING SEAT BELTS

When about wearing seat belts? It may be a waste of time to suggest it, but the safe rule is to wear them. (It does mean the couple can't sit as close together as they would like. (Using driver and passenger in one seat belt doesn't work well.) But wearing seat belts might insure that they are able to go out on another date.

MANNERS ON A DATE

We have to draw a fine line between a girl being either a clinging vine or too independent. This is true for women of all ages. Of course a girl is able to open a door by herself, and get in and out of a car unaided, and carry her own suitcase, and ring for the elevator herself. And there are times when she may properly do these things even when accompanied by a man. If it is impossible for a man to come around and open the car door for his date to get out, it would be silly for her to sit there helpless. We always have to use common sense about these things.

But waiting for a man to be courteous helps him to *be* courteous. It gives the girl the feeling of being looked after, and lets the man assume his rightful place of responsibility and leadership in their relationship. This same principle should be carried on through married life.

INVITING A DATE IN

Whether a man is invited into the house after a date or not, he gets out of the car, goes around to open the car door for the girl, and takes her to her door. If she

1

PERSONAL BEHAVIOR AND TABLE MANNERS

The wise man wrote: "Keep thy heart with all diligence; for out of it are the issues of life" (Proverbs 4:23). Anyone can learn and automatically follow etiquette rules. But there must be an inner acceptance of the rule as well as outward conformity to it if we are to really obey the command of Scripture to be "sincere and without offence" in our behavior (Philippians 1:10).

PERSONAL APPEARANCE

Personal appearance is the place to begin any discussion of manners and behavior. Before we say or do anything, we are judged by appearance alone. This is unfair, since a person's character is not based on clean fingernails, pressed clothes and the ability to make introductions correctly. A fine appearance may mask a ruthless tyrant, while one who is not up on all the fine points of etiquette may have the essence of good manners, which is consideration for others. Yet the Scripture reminds us in I Samuel 16:7 that "man looketh on the outward appearance." Since we cannot see a man's integrity, we can only judge him by his behavior. This is one reason personal appearance and manners are an important part of etiquette. Fortunately it is possible to have both inner character and correct outward behavior.

CLEANLINESS

Cleanliness is the first essential in personal etiquette. Scrupulously clean hair, skin, teeth and clothes are possible for everyone, because they do not depend on age or beauty or the amount of money in the bank. Good grooming is more than a dressing table stocked with creams and lotions and a closet full of expensive clothing. It includes a daily bath, regular shampooing, the use of deodorants, and clean, well-pressed clothes. Too often women use perfume as a cover-up when it should only enhance already clean skin. Men need to pay attention to these details too if they want to be welcomed by others. In recent years there has been an increasing trend toward the use of lotions and cologne by men and, when used with restraint, they are an aid to good grooming.

WOMEN'S DRESS

Personal etiquette has to do also with the way we dress. Our more relaxed, casual living has changed what formerly were inexorable standards in personal appearance especially for women. Naturally, few women feel like dressing up just to dash to the store for a loaf of bread or to run out to the corner mailbox. Yet the old advice of not attracting attention to oneself in public is valid even in our era of casualness in dress and appearance. It isn't the purpose of this chapter to criticize certain styles. It is true that the mini-skirt attracts attention on the street, but so would a dress of the 1880's if worn to the supermarket. A woman must use common sense and good taste in dress, and take pride in her appearance when going out among other people.

CONTEMPORARY STYLES

Today's styles provide such a variety of women's clothing which is casual and yet attractive, dressy and yet not expensive, that no one need be sloppy in appearance. Women particularly need the reminder of Robert Burns' words about seeing ourselves as others see us, to keep from appearing in public in any old thing; and the older a woman gets, the more she should heed the advice.

A well-dressed woman wears clothing that is suit-able for what she is doing because certain clothes are right for one time and place and are not right for another. We wear a bathing suit when we swim and a dress when we eat dinner and we don't reverse the order. Sometimes wearing slacks or a divided skirt to garden or to hike is more appropriate than wearing a dress.

COMMUNITY STANDARDS

A well-dressed woman also tries to fit the pattern of dress in the community in which she lives. Women whose husbands are transferred frequently for busi-ness reasons find that what is acceptable in one part of the country is not proper in another place. There may be a great gulf fixed between what is proper dress in

Boston and what is acceptable in San Francisco, and these community standards can't be ignored.

But even conformity to a community standard must be conditioned by individual good taste. Just because everyone wears a particular style or does a certain thing, does not mean that it is right for every person. Good taste in dress means using good sense to decide what looks best on us personally. We must know what we can wear well and not be swayed by the vagaries of fashion decrees, especially when we remember that these are not made in the interest of the general public, but to make money for the fashion industry.

Perhaps the basic rule that will always keep a person well dressed is to be up-to-date and yet not extreme. There is a middle road that most of us would do well to follow. Alexander Pope said, "Be not the first by whom the new is tried, nor yet the last to lay the old aside." For women this applies to makeup and hair styles as well as to clothing. Simplicity is always in good taste and in right style, both in dress and accessories.

A CHRISTIAN WOMAN'S STANDARDS

The Christian woman has an even deeper motivation to be careful of her appearance since she is a citizen of another world and is responsible to her Lord who has commanded: "Be not conformed to this world . . . be transformed" (Romans 12:2). This does not refer directly to personal appearance, and yet we can apply the principle, which is not to follow the world's standards when they conflict with God's standards of holiness. None of us wants to be dowdy or out of style, and that is why we often put aside our own good judgment and are swept along with the current fad regardless of what it is.

A Christian woman's dress and appearance are not to be colorless and old-fashioned, but they must be modest. It is true that there is wide latitude in this and a definite rule cannot be made for everyone. There are times when an outfit which covers one from head to foot can be less modest than a sleeveless short dress. This must remain an individual matter in which a woman retains a sense of objectivity in deciding what is becoming to her, is suitable to the occasion and place, and is within the limits of propriety as she reads God's Word and maintains a Christian witness.

This is not easy to do in our day of shifting moral values. Some may think that God's standard of personal holiness is too high for our generation to follow. But this standard (I Corinthians 6:19-20) was originally given to a group of believers who lived in a city which was synonymous with evil. God's command that His children be in but not of the world has never changed.

WEARING HATS, GLOVES

We find that today's styles in dress often do not follow yesterday's conventions. For example, women wear hats much less frequently than used to be the custom. This is true even in many churches where hats are seldom worn in the Sunday evening service and often not in the morning service. Yet hats are in good taste almost anywhere and on almost any occasion except with an evening dress. A hat is always correct when worn to church, to an afternoon tea, at a reception or anyplace else you may want to wear one.

Gloves are still generally worn and are proper anyplace and at any time except an informal occasion such as a picnic or barbecue, for they give a costume a finished look and, of course, keep the hands warm and clean. It isn't necessary to remove a glove to shake hands nor to apologize for not doing so, although gloves are always removed at the table before eating.

It is always safer to err on the side of not wearing enough jewelry than too much. This is true of wearing makeup also. Fashion experts every so often hail the natural look as being right for a particular season. Actually this should always be the goal in using cosmetics.

MEN'S CLOTHING

Men's clothing styles have not changed as rapidly or as frequently as have women's, though we are now seeing more new experiments in men's fashions. Though styles change slowly, they do change, and a man should keep up with them. To wear a double-breasted coat when everyone else is wearing single-breasted, or to wear a suit with wide lapels because it is still good even though the current style is for narrow lapels, is not good taste. There must be some conformity to the dress of the group with which a man lives and works—even though he must do what is right for him within the framework of his surroundings—or he will be considered an eccentric. For the Christian who must live his witness in an alien world (Philippians 2:15), it is important that this witness not be ridiculed by his being unnecessarily old-fashioned and out-of-date.

A well-dressed man's clothes fit well, they are appropriate to the occasion and place where they are worn, and they suit his personality. Casual clothes are sometimes more expensive than a suit, but this does not mean such clothes are proper for a funeral or a wedding or an important business conference. There is comfort in knowing that there is no one right way to dress. Some men would not feel comfortable in a colored shirt; others prefer light colors or stripes. Non-matching trousers and coats were unheard of a few years ago but now they are worn in many offices. It is best to follow the style of your office, since some places allow shirt sleeves on a hot day while others demand a suit coat at all times. (For a discussion of formal clothes, see the chapter on Weddings.)

Current styles affect even the wearing of a handkerchief in the suit coat breast pocket. Sometimes the handkerchief is white, sometimes colored; often it is folded square and again it is folded with several points showing. The man who lives and works among other men to whom small details like this would be considered an affectation probably would not bother with them either. But the one who mingles with those to whom these details are important would be wise to consider them important too.

MEN'S JEWELRY

Wearing jewelry is an individual matter. Some men would never wear a ring other than a wedding ring, while to others this is a necessary item. In our day more men's jewelry is coming on the market. We must remember that in past cultures men wore more jewelry than they have in recent decades. Then for many years jewelry was considered effeminate and men did not even wear wristwatches until World War I. This is an individual matter based on personal preference and many other factors.

A well-groomed man is clean and properly shaved, his hair is cut when necessary to keep it neat depending on how he chooses to wear it, his shoes are polished and his clothes are pressed. It is impossible to set hard and fast rules about clothing and appearance other than to give the reminder that extremes are usually a poor investment both in money and in the impression made on others.

But etiquette governs more than just personal appearance. Certain forms of behavior have developed through the years which are designed to make living with others easier and happier.

COURTESIES BETWEEN MEN AND WOMEN

It is customary for a man to walk on the curbside of the street when he is with a woman. This comes from a past era when protection was needed from runaway horses or garbage thrown from windows overhead. But walking on the curbside is not a firm rule any longer, though we are so accustomed to the habit that a man who doesn't do so might be thought either rude or ignorant. When a man is with two women, it is better for him to walk on the curbside rather than between them simply because it is easier to carry on a conversation with both of them from this position.

This is an example of how a rule of etiquette can be looked at from a commonsense viewpoint and adjusted when necessary.

WHEN A MAN PRECEDES A WOMAN

Generally a man precedes a woman at any time there might be danger or when he is not sure of the situation ahead. A woman gets into a car or taxi first, but the man gets out first in order to help her out. He goes first down a steep staircase, and he gets off a train or bus first so that he is there to help her as she steps down. Such help should be accepted by a woman with a gracious thank you, even though there are many times when she has no escort and still manages to get along. Many women discourage such courtesies in men because they accept them as their due rather than being grateful for the polite attention.

A woman ordinarily goes through a door before a man, including a revolving door which he starts in motion for her. However when walking through a train a man would go first in order to open the heavy doors between the cars. There is another time when a man may correctly go ahead of a woman and this is when getting off a crowded elevator. It is better from the standpoint of both speed and safety for men to get off an elevator first when they are nearest the doors, than to shift back and forth to allow all the women to precede them.

WHEN TO REMOVE ONE'S HAT

While a man always removes his hat indoors, except in stores and in halls of public buildings, it is sometimes necessary to leave it on in an elevator since it takes up less room when worn than when held. A man lifts his hat when meeting a woman he knows and removes it entirely if he stops to talk to her. It is also removed at a committal service at a cemetery, when the national anthem is played, and when the flag is carried by.

OFFERING A SEAT

It has been traditional that a man offer his seat on a crowded bus or train to a woman who is standing. Today this should certainly be done for an elderly woman or for a mother who is holding a young child. It is a courtesy that parents can instill in young sons and daughters. However, in our day of equality in the working world, a tired business girl should not expect that an equally tired businessman stand so that she might sit. Naturally a child for whom no fare has been paid should not occupy a seat by himself if adults are standing.

KEEPING PUBLIC PLACES CLEAN

It is a strange quirk of human nature that a normally polite person can become rude and ill-mannered in a public place without seeming to be aware of his discourteous behavior. People who are clean at home, when traveling leave public washrooms in a filthy condition. Signs have to be put up in public places to warn people against spitting or throwing chewing gum and papers on the floors and grass. Those who talk through a concert are rude both to the performer and to others in the audience.

CHURCH BEHAVIOR

Even in church, people are sometimes ill-mannered. The Apostle Paul reminds Timothy of the necessity of knowing "how thou oughtest to behave thyself in the house of God, which is the church of the living God" (I Timothy 3:15). Many people need the reminder that they do not come to church to visit with friends but to worship. Coming in quietly, sitting down for a moment of silent prayer, listening quietly to the prelude, help to establish an attitude of worship. Friendliness to strangers may be shown by speaking to them after the service; before, a smile of welcome is enough. When attending a service in a church of another faith, it is not necessary to follow all the ritual unless one wishes to. Generally speaking however in a Catholic service one kneels to pray; a Protestant certainly can do this. It is not necessary to take communion in a church other than one's own. In fact, many churches have rules governing the taking of communion so that only those who are members may partake. In Catholic churches women must wear some kind of head covering, and in Jewish synagogues men must have their heads covered.

TABLE MANNERS

Any discussion of personal etiquette must also consider table manners, for many people give offense here when they have no intention of doing so. The one who feels that the way he eats is his own business probably ought always to eat by himself. Table manners have changed through the years, but those that have endured are based on consideration for others. We have come a long way from the days when all food was eaten in the fingers and scraps were thrown under the table for the dogs to fight over. Correct table manners have to do with how we look to others while eating, and how they look to us. If we try watching ourselves in a mirror while eating, we will better understand the reasons for some of the rules.

There are times, of course, when the rules are relaxed. It's all right to read the newspaper when you're eating by yourself, and to put your elbows on the table at home after dinner while talking, and to omit the underplate for the baby's soup bowl. But knowing correct table manners gives us self-confidence when we are in places where we will be judged by our manners. And the only way to be sure of doing things right when it matters is to practice manners daily.

USE OF KNIFE AND FORK

Cultural differences show up in table manners more than in some other areas of etiquette. An example of this is in the use of the knife and fork. There is the American style, which is the zigzag method of transferring the knife and fork from one hand to the other while cutting and eating food. The fork is held in the left hand with the prongs down and the handle pressed against the palm of the hand, and the knife is held in the right hand while the food is cut. Then the knife is laid across the top edge of the plate, the fork is transferred to the right hand, and the food is lifted to the mouth with the prongs of the fork up. Since only several bites of meat are supposed to be cut at one time, this makes for constant motion. In the Continental style used in England and in Europe, the fork remains in the left hand and the knife in the right throughout the meal. The food, piled on the back of the fork, is carried to the mouth with the prongs of the fork down. Either method or a combination is equally acceptable. Whatever method is used, the main thing in eating is to do so as neatly, quietly and inconspicuously as possible.

DON'TS IN TABLE MANNERS

There are some don'ts that must be included in any discussion of table manners. These include not putting a used, wet teaspoon in the sugar bowl or one's own used knife in the butter dish, reaching across someone's plate to get food from a serving dish, talking with the mouth full of food, hunching over one's plate as though afraid it will be snatched away, bringing the head down to the plate to eat rather than lifting the food to the mouth, chewing loudly or with the mouth open, pushing the plate away when one has finished a course, washing down food with a beverage. These are some of the most common errors and those most offensive to others.

One should sit straight at the table with elbows held near the sides to avoid bumping people on either side. Silverware is never put on the tablecloth after it has been used nor planked on the edge of the plate with the handle on the cloth. Instead, the knife after use is placed across the upper edge of the plate with the cutting side facing inward. When passing the plate for another serving, leave both the knife and fork on the plate close together in the center so that they will not fall off.

WHEN TO BEGIN EATING

It isn't necessary to wait until everyone at the table has been served before beginning to eat, particularly at a large dinner. It is more sensible to begin as soon as those nearby have been served in order to keep the food from getting cold. When there are only a few at the table, of course one should wait for the hostess to begin.

EATING CERTAIN FOODS

Eating quietly without calling attention to ourselves is the aim of good table manners, but this is sometimes difficult to do, particularly with certain foods. Fried chicken is an example of this, because picking it up in the fingers is perfectly correct in certain situations but not in others, and the problem is to know which is which. When eating as a family or with a group of close friends or on a picnic, most of us feel quite at ease to pick up the chicken bone and eat the meat from it. Many restaurants which specialize in serving chicken do so with the understanding that it is to be eaten in the fingers. However, to assume that it is always correct to do so may make for embarrassing situations. This is one time when it is safest to wait and see what the hostess does. When no one seems to know what to do, it's a good idea to cut as much of the meat off the bone as possible before picking it up. Corn on the cob is another delicious food that can't be eaten daintily by anyone. But don't make the mistake of buttering the whole ear at once, settling elbows on the table and going after it. It's better to put butter on a small section at a time and eat it as quietly as possible.

Naturally a whole slice of bread is not picked up and buttered all at once. Instead, a small piece at a time is broken off and buttered.

Knowing where to put relishes is sometimes a problem. Generally, anything which is eaten with a fork along with meat and potatoes goes on the dinner plate—cranberry sauce, piccalilli, catsup. Anything that is eaten with the fingers or put on bread goes on the salad plate or on the bread and butter plate. This would include olives, celery, strips of pickle, and jelly or preserves. In this connection remember that salt which is to be dipped into, for celery for example, must be put on a plate and not on the table.

Any food that is soft or sticky should be eaten with a fork. Sometimes cake is dry enough to be eaten in the fingers and sometimes a fork is needed. Food should never be dunked, no matter how dry it is, unless you are eating alone with no one to observe the messy process.

Most of the rules regarding the how of eating certain foods are really very practical for ease in eating without being messy. For example, french fried potatoes are better eaten with a fork because they do leave the fingers greasy. Bacon should be cut with a fork unless it is very dry and crisp, and then it can be picked up in the fingers. If one is able successfully to wind long strands of spaghetti around a fork which is held against the bowl of a spoon, fine; otherwise it's best to cut it with a fork. This is true of eating salads also, for sometimes lettuce must be cut with a knife to make it easier to eat.

Fried shrimp, if they are small, can be eaten whole with a fork; otherwise they should be cut in half. Large shrimp when served as a first course may be eaten, a biteful at a time, from a fork since they are difficult to cut in a small, stemmed glass.

Various kinds of berries are eaten with a spoon unless they are large strawberries which are served whole with a bowl of powdered sugar. Then they are picked up by the stem, dipped in the sugar, eaten in the fingers, and the stem laid on a plate.

Pits from food are removed from the mouth in the same way the food is eaten. For example, an olive is eaten by holding it in the fingers and biting around the stone which is then laid on a plate. Canned cherries are put in the mouth, the fruit eaten off and the stone put into a spoon and then laid on the plate.

Soup is spooned away from one and sipped quietly from the side of the spoon without slurping noises. When clear soup is served in a cup with handles, it is correct to pick it up and drink the soup when it is cool enough to do so. Whether soup is served in a cup or in a soup bowl there should be an underplate, and this is where the soup spoon is put when one has finished using it. It should not be left sticking out of the cup or bowl.

Perhaps a word should be said about what to do when you know the rules and the one who set the table obviously did not. Perhaps there is no underplate for the soup bowl and so there is no place to put the spoon. Or there is no butter knife and your own knife has already been used to cut another food. This is where the basic rule of good manners—consideration for others—is important. You leave the spoon in the cup, or go ahead and use your own knife, because in this instance it's the courteous thing to do. This principle applies in many other situations. It's never polite to call attention to someone else's mistake.

If something is spilled at the table it should be wiped up quickly and quietly with as little fuss as possible made over it by either guest or hostess. Accidents can happen to anyone and it isn't necessary to be too profuse in apologizing.

NAPKINS, FINGER BOWLS

Small napkins are opened all the way when placed on the lap, otherwise they are not of much value. Larger ones are opened only halfway, and are never tucked in at the neck even at the risk of spilling food on one's tie or dress. It should be possible to eat in small enough bites not to splatter food even when eating drippy foods such as spaghetti. At the end of a meal the napkin is left lying loosely unfolded at the side of the plate. Paper napkins should not be crumpled into a tight ball.

Finger bowls have been considered a part only of formal entertaining and have even been thought of by some as an affectation. Actually they are a practical and sometimes necessary convenience, particularly if fruit or sticky food has been served as the dessert. If used, finger bowls are brought to the table with the dessert. The fingers are dipped in, one hand at a time, and dried on the napkin. This can save the napkins from bad stains. In this connection, women should always be careful not to leave lipstick stains on cloth napkins.

DIETING

We are all diet conscious these days, but this shouldn't become a topic of conversation at the dinner table because it isn't as interesting to others as it is to the dieter. If one is on a very strict diet or is allergic to certain foods, it is perhaps better not to accept invitations to meals. Otherwise, one can take a small amount of what is served without giving a detailed description of one's diet. The same rule applies when we are faced with foods we dislike. If we are eating with a large group, we can simply either not take any of a certain food or leave most of it if it has already been served on the plate. At a small dinner party it may be necessary to eat the food whether we want to or not. Sometimes dislike of liver or artichokes or oysters comes from not having eaten them enough to get used to them. Learning to eat a variety of foods is part of the social adaptability most of us need to develop to a greater degree.

SAYING GRACE

When God's blessing on the food is asked, it is usually done at the beginning of the meal before anyone has begun to eat. In some homes a grace is also said at the end of the meal. The guest who is not used to the custom of table grace will be spared embarrassment if he waits to begin eating until the hostess gives the signal. The blessing is asked either by the host or hostess, by one of the children, or by a guest if the host is sure he will want to and will not be embarrassed at being asked.

The same table rules apply when eating in a restaurant as when eating at home. The main point is always to avoid being conspicuous in any way. This rules out loud talking and laughing, calling to others across the room, punishing children at the table, repairing make-up (never use a comb at the table either at home or in public) and scolding a waiter for any reason.

Then won't saying grace before a meal in a public place make one conspicuous? Not if it is done as naturally and as quietly as though one were at home. When dining alone or with the family or a group of friends, it is a simple matter for each one to bow his head in silent thanks, or even for one person to offer a prayer aloud quietly. When eating with a group where bowing in prayer would seem to be for appearance only or be interpreted as an implied criticism of those who do not pray, thanks can be offered from the heart, which God sees, without bowing outwardly. After all, asking a blessing on the food is an expression of thankfulness to God, not a witness to one's Christian faith. If it is done just to impress others with one's piety, then it should not be done. The one who asks God's blessing on his food in public and does so reverently and without ostentation need not be bothered by someone else's criticism.

RESTAURANT MANNERS

There are some rules which apply when eating in a restaurant which are not true when eating in a home. In a restaurant men either check their hats and coats or hang them on the coatrack. Women may do so if they like, but they generally prefer to keep their coats on until they are seated and then lay them back over the chair. When entering a restaurant, a couple waits for the headwaiter or hostess to show them to a table with the woman going first. If there is no hostess, the man goes first to a table, pulls out a chair for the woman and pushes it in slowly as she sits down. She sits across from her escort and has the choice seat, either facing the room and the other diners or the view through the window. When two couples are together in a booth, the women sit next to the wall with the men on the outside. A woman always puts her purse and gloves in her lap, never on the table. If the purse is too large to fit comfortably on her lap, it may be set on the floor.

ORDERING A MEAL

In ordering, a woman chooses what she would like and tells her escort, who then gives the order with his own to the waiter. This procedure is true for a young couple on a date, a husband and wife having dinner, or a mother dining out with her teenage son. The only time a woman would give her own order is when dining with a large group and the waiter asks for individual orders to avoid confusion.

A woman should always be considerate of her escort's wallet. If she knows that he can well afford a high-priced dinner, she should feel free to order it. If she isn't sure what he can afford at that particular time, she could either order a medium-priced dinner, or first ask what appeals to him and then choose from the price range his choice indicates.

An a la carte menu (by the bill of fare) means that one orders from a list of foods each of which is priced separately, sometimes including the bread and butter and beverage. This is fine if one wants only one or two courses, but it is more expensive when one orders a full dinner. Table d'hôte (from the host's table) means that a set price is listed for the complete dinner and usually includes the appetizer, salad, entrée, vegetables, dessert and beverage. Or a menu will indicate a price after each entrée (main course) and this means that the price also includes the appetizer, salad, dessert and beverage. When a menu doesn't give prices, this usually means the prices are high. Order anyway provided money doesn't matter to you. But in this case you may always ask for a menu that does list the prices. If you find that you can't afford to eat there, just get up quietly and leave. If the waiter has already brought water, explain that you've changed your mind and don't wish to be served after all. Naturally there will be some embarrassment but not as much as there would be if you went ahead and ate and then couldn't pay for the meal.

Since a man always must rise and remain standing as long as a woman is standing, women should be careful about stopping in a restaurant to visit with friends who are already eating. It is rude for two women to chat about inconsequentials while a man's dinner grows cold.

PAYING, TIPPING

When a couple has finished dinner, the man asks the waiter for the check which is brought face downward on a tray or laid face down on the table. A group of people dining together who intend to pay their own way should either have separate checks or should let one person pay the bill with the others settling accounts later. This avoids on-the-spot haggling over who had what at what price.

If the waiter is paid, he will return the change on a tray, and that is where the tip is left. If the check is paid to the cashier, the tip for the waiter is left in plain sight on the table. If you do not have enough change, get it when the bill is paid and return with it to the table immediately. Many people are finding it increasingly convenient to use a credit card to pay for meals, especially when traveling. In this case it is usually better to leave the tip just as though you were paying cash.

The standard for tipping in a restaurant is 15 percent of the bill. If the service has been poor or even just average, no more than that is required. If the service has been unusually good or you have required extra attention, you may want to tip more generously. When the bill for a larger group means that 15 percent amounts to more than two or three dollars, then 10 percent is enough. Some people feel that it isn't necessary to tip when they have eaten at a counter and perhaps had only a cup of coffee and a piece of pie. But if the girl wiped off the counter and brought a glass of water and a napkin, and especially if she did it with a smile, a small tip would show appreciation.

LEAVING TRACTS

A special word of caution is needed about leaving tracts. If you or your party have been demanding in the service required, or if someone in the group has been rude or faultfinding, or if you do not leave an adequate tip (by the waiter's standards, not yours), it would be better not to leave a tract. Your behavior would already have taken away the value of a written witness. But when a tract is left, it should be one that leaves an appropriate message. The kind that begins with gracious thanks for the service is more apt to be read than the one that warns immediately of judgment to come.

WHEN A WOMAN PAYS THE CHECK

There are occasions when a woman pays her own way in a restaurant. This is true for a coffee break or lunch when a girl is joined by a man who is a friend but not a date. She should not expect him to pay her way just because they are eating together, nor should he feel obligated to do so. (The same principle applies when a girl regularly rides a bus or train to work. A man friend who rides regularly with her does not pay her fare.)

A woman in business sometimes takes a man client out to lunch and is, of course, responsible for the check. Sometimes a single girl would like to entertain friends for dinner and finds it more convenient to take them to a restaurant. In these situations it is always embarrassing for a man to sit by while a woman pays for a meal for them both. There are several ways of avoiding such embarrassments. The woman may make arrangements with the restaurant in advance to be billed for the meal. Or she may take the group or client to a restaurant where she is known and can just sign the check. Or she may give money to the man ahead of time so that he ostensibly pays the bill. When a mother is dining with a teenage son, his ego would be helped and he would gain valuable social experience if the latter method were followed with him.

Etiquette demands that consideration be shown to everyone regardless of who he is. Unfortunately there are people who are considerate of and courteous only to those whom they want to impress, and are rude and impolite to waiters, cab drivers, elevator operators, clerks and others who serve them. This is really a sign of personal insecurity. True courtesy which is based on consideration for others "vaunteth not itself, is not puffed up" (I Corinthians 13:4). There is never an excuse for rudeness to anyone no matter how justified we might feel.

REFUSING A DRINK OR A CIGARETTE

Rudeness appears in many forms though it sometimes may be unintentional. One form of rudeness is seen in those who offer and those who refuse cigarettes and liquor. Even though the medical profession warns against the bad effects of cigarettes and alcohol, almost everyone from time to time finds himself being offered one or the other, sometimes insistently, and there is needless embarrassment about refusing. The person who needs support in his refusal can find it in medical statistics. However, it is never necessary to be apologetic in refusing a cigarette or a drink or to give elaborate excuses. A simple, "No, thank you" with a smile is enough. After all, no one bothers to explain at great length why he does not care for a drink of tomato juice or apologize for not taking orange juice before dinner. The same principle can be applied to refusing any other kind of drink.

Nor is it necessary, when refusing, to launch into a lecture on the evils of drinking and smoking, or to attack and condemn those who do. This will not win anyone over to your viewpoint. Naturally if asked to give a reason for refusing, one should be able to state his convictions politely but positively. It is well to remember that some Christians do smoke with a clear conscience and do not equate Christianity and cigarettes, and in some countries drinking wine is acceptable in Christian circles. Each one is responsible to God for his behavior in this matter and one can keep one's own convictions without condemning others for theirs.

Responsibility to God is really the touchstone for the Christian as he thinks of etiquette rules in personal living. It is important that we be personally acceptable to others; if they do not like us, they will not like our message. But no one can please everyone always; so, in the last analysis, acceptability with God is the standard for the Christian's code of conduct. If we really love God with all our heart, soul, mind and body, and our neighbor as ourselves, rules of proper behavior will not be a problem.

2

INTRODUCTIONS

Ecclesiastes 3:7 reminds that there is a "time to keep silence, and a time to speak." When we do not know just what to say when meeting people, we either say too little or too much. The purpose of an introduction is to help acquaint one person with another as a first step to friendship. This is one area where there is needless confusion about what to do, simply because we try too hard to remember the forms and forget the fundamental rule of good manners, which is consideration for others.

CORRECT ORDER

The basic rules for making introductions are quite simple. The main point to remember is that the less honored person is presented *to* the more honored person. This is sometimes just a matter of ladies first when introducing a man to a woman. It also shows respect for the more important person by implying that he is already known and does not need to be introduced to anyone else. That is why a younger person is presented to an older person, a child to an adult, a man to a woman (with certain exceptions, of course, such as when the man is the President), friends to parents, people without titles to those with titles.

Sometimes one's own personal feelings are ignored in this matter. For example, you may rightly feel that your father is the most important man in the world, but you would nonetheless introduce him to a United States senator or to the mayor of the city. Respect for the office is involved here.

Following this basic rule, you *first* mention the name of the person to whom respect is being shown. For example:

> Mrs. Eighty, may I present Miss Sixteen?
> Mother, this is Sally Company.
> Miss Black, have you met Mr. White?
> Mother and Dad, this is Jim and Mary Friend.
> General Two Stars, this is Private First Class.

Of course, if the wrong name slips out first, it is easy to correct it smoothly by saying, "Miss Sixteen, I'd like you to meet Mrs. Eighty." One can also just mention the two names in the right order as, "Miss Black–Mr. White," though it takes only a moment longer to say the few extra words which make for a more gracious introduction. When just the names are used, it isn't necessary to repeat them twice: "Miss Black–Mr. White; Mr. White–Miss Black." If for some reason your mind goes blank and you can't remember any rule of how to introduce properly, this isn't too serious a problem. Give the names anyway because being friendly is more important than being correct. Then resolve to remember this one basic rule of showing respect to a person because of age, sex or position.

FAMILY MEMBERS

A wife introduces and speaks of her husband to friends as "John," to casual acquaintances as "my husband," but never as "Mr. Smith" when she is speaking of him socially. The same is true of a husband when introducing and speaking of his wife. He should not say "the wife" but "my wife." Sons and daughters are always introduced to others as one's children unless the name is different. If a daughter is married, one would say, "Mrs. Smith, this is my daughter, Mrs. Married." If there is some other reason why the child's name is different it could be mentioned if necessary, but the initial introduction is, "My son, John" or "My daughter, Mary." Other family members are referred to as "my sister," "my father," "my aunt."

CLERGYMEN

A Protestant minister is not introduced as "Reverend Smith" because the word reverend is an adjective and should not be coupled with a person's name. He is presented as "Mr. Smith, the pastor of Forest Avenue Church," if you want to indicate that he is a minister. If he has a degree, he would be introduced as "Dr. Smith." A Catholic speaks of his priest as "Father," and a Jewish rabbi is addressed as "Rabbi."

DEGREES, ACADEMIC TITLES

Doctors and dentists are usually introduced by their title instead of Mr. An earned or an honorary degree in other areas is always used professionally. But in private life a man with a degree other than medical does not use his title in speaking of himself. Of course, his friends may do so out of courtesy and respect for the degree. We should have at least a passing acquaintance with academic titles. Earned degrees include the Ph.D. (doctor of philosophy) and the Th.D. (doctor of theology). Honorary degrees are the D.D. (doctor of divinity), LL.D. (doctor of laws), Litt.D. (doctor of letters) and Sc.D. (doctor of science). A person who holds any of these degrees is introduced and spoken to by others as "Dr." though he would not introduce himself in that way. Those in administrative positions in a school would be introduced as "President" or "Dean," or would be called "Dr." if they have a degree. The instructional titles on most campuses are Professor, Associate Professor, Assistant Professor, Instructor and Assistant. The first three are usually all introduced as "Professor." While a man does not use his title in speaking of himself, it is a mark of respect for the individual if others are familiar with his title and use it properly.

GOVERNMENT AND MILITARY TITLES

Most of us feel that we can manage pretty well the ordinary introductions and greetings, but are not quite sure how to introduce and address people with titles. There was a time when the average citizen never expected to meet the President or a United States senator or the lord mayor of a city in England. But now we travel farther from home and are more likely to find ourselves shaking hands with a governor or a foreign diplomat than we ever thought possible.

It would be impossible to remember the correct title

of every person whose path we are likely to cross. But there are certain representative titles that we can learn. The one who plans to travel should make this a part of his plans and check the protocol of the countries he expects to visit.

The President of the United States is introduced either by that full title or as "the President," and is spoken to as "Mr. President." The Vice-President is introduced by his title only, but may be addressed either as "Mr. Vice-President" or by his name, "Mr. Smith." Cabinet members are called "Mr. Secretary," but when introduced the full title should be given: "The Secretary of Labor, Mr. Smith." A United States senator or representative is introduced as "Senator" or "Representative Smith" from such and such a state. In writing to them they are addressed as "The Honorable John Smith, United States Senate" or "United States House of Representatives." In fact, the term "the Honorable" may be used correctly with any of our elected officials or ambassadors. State senators and representatives are introduced and addressed in the same way. A governor is always spoken of as "Governor Smith" or "the Governor." A mayor is introduced as "Mayor Smith," and is spoken to either in that way or as "Mr. Mayor." The wives of government officials are addressed as "Mrs." and are not included in their husband's title. One does not say, "Senator Smith and Mrs. Senator Smith" but "Senator and Mrs. Smith."

Usually ambassadors are referred to as "the Ambassador" of such and such a country, although there are a few exceptions. It is well to remember that our ambassador in Central or South America is not called "the American Ambassador," but "the Ambassador of the United States," since citizens in those countries are Americans also.

The official use of military titles involves a good bit of protocol which simply has to be learned. But in introducing military people socially, the general rule is that all colonels are called "Colonel," and all lieutenants are "Lieutenant," and so on regardless of the rank. This is true of other branches of the service as well. However, the title is always used with the man's name when referring to him, as "Lieutenant Smith"; never use the title by itself. All officers keep their rank after retiring.

Chaplains in the armed services are addressed as "Chaplain" regardless of their military rank. Officers in the National Guard and the Reserves use their titles only when they are on active duty. When rank is used, it must have the proper designation with it. For example, Lieutenant Smith's name would be followed by letters designating which reserve he is in whether NG (National Guard), USAR (United States Army Reserve), USNR (United States Naval Reserve), USMC (United States Marine Corps), USAF (United States Air Force) or USCG (United States Coast Guard).

GROUP INTRODUCTIONS

An individual may be introduced to a group in the order in which people are sitting or standing, rather than trying first to introduce the older people or to skip around the circle picking out all the women first. One may either give the individual's name and then go around the group in order, or get the attention of each person separately and then give the stranger's name. However, it isn't really necessary to repeat the individual's name each time when giving group introductions. If it isn't convenient to introduce to the entire group, just mention the guest's name to a few who are nearby and let them introduce him to others. He will probably not remember all the names anyway if they are given all at once, and this way he will remember a few. Naturally if the guest is the one whom the group has met to honor, then there will be individual introductions, since everyone will want to meet him personally. It is not always necessary in a large group to introduce every guest. At an open house, for example, where people come and go over a period of time, it is impossible to formally introduce everyone.

TEENAGE INTRODUCTIONS

Informality among teenage introductions is to be expected and is all right as long as they know when to be properly formal. A casual "Hi, everyone, I want you to meet Sally Smith" is a friendly and natural teenage introduction. The titles "Miss," "Mrs." and "Mr." are usually not used when young people introduce each other.

HOW TO INTRODUCE AND REPLY

A simple form of introduction is "May I present?" An even less formal form is "May I introduce?" or "I'd like you to meet." Other forms are correct of course, depending on the situation. As has already been said, young people would probably never say,

"May I present?" One can also say, "Do you know?" or "Have you met?" or "This is," etc.

There are certain expressions which should not be used when making introductions. "Shake hands with," "I want to make you acquainted with" or "Meet my friend" (as though the other person were not a friend) are definitely out.

The simplest and always correct answer to an introduction is "How do you do?" said with a smile. If you show genuine warmth in your tone of voice and smile, it will be appreciated and you will be more easily remembered by the other person. If possible repeat the person's name to help fix it in your mind. In our more casual day the response to an introduction is often "Hello" or even "Hi." But "How do you do?" is always correct in any situation and can be warm and sincere and friendly. Young people especially should learn to respond in this way at least occasionally, to keep them from a breathless and immature "Hi" when meeting someone of importance whom they would really like to impress.

Other answers such as "Pleased to meet you," "I'm glad to know you" (which isn't true since you have just met), "Charmed" are taboo. When parting after an introduction, one says, "I'm glad to have met you," and the answer may be just "Thank you" or "I'm glad to have met *you*," with the tone of voice carrying the burden of proof.

The person whose name is mentioned first is supposed to answer first. But if he doesn't, go ahead and acknowledge the introduction anyway. It isn't necessary to stand on that much formality; anyway, friend-

liness should come first whenever we meet and talk
with others. Many people really don't know how to
handle and reply to introductions, so that what seems
to be unfriendliness is often just the result of ignor-
ance rather than deliberate rudeness.

Since one purpose of an introduction is to make
strangers feel less like strangers to each other, a clearly
spoken name with at least a minimum of information
is a necessity. For example, "Mrs. Smith, I'd like you
to meet Mrs. Jones who has just moved here from San
Francisco." Accurate information is important too
when introducing in-laws. To introduce your husband's mother as "Mother" because you feel that close
an affection for her, is nice; but it is confusing to
others who will assume she is your mother. It is better
to say simply, "My mother-in-law, Mrs. Jones" or
"This is Dick's mother." Actually it is the tone of voice
which makes or breaks an introduction, for the voice
may express warmth, affection, rivalry, indifference or
positive dislike.

SHAKING HANDS

A man always rises when he is introduced to either
a woman or another man, and always shakes hands
with a man. A hostess also rises and shakes hands
when greeting each guest, whether man or woman, as
an extra expression of welcome, and she does the
same when guests leave. Younger women usually
rise when introduced to an older woman or when an
older woman stops to speak to them. Probably some
caution should be used here and a younger woman
should stand only for someone who is obviously

older. Even very elderly women don't like to have that much attention called to their age.

A woman has the privilege of shaking hands or not when she is introduced. However, if the other person, whether man or woman, holds out his hand, she should by all means shake it and do so firmly, for no one likes a limp handshake. This is another one of those times when a form of etiquette is ignored in favor of politeness and consideration. It isn't necessary to remove one's glove at any time to shake hands, not even when leaving church and greeting the minister.

INTRODUCING ONESELF

In this matter of introductions one sometimes meets situations which can be embarrassing. If you are standing by someone you don't know and no one offers to introduce you, a friendly "Hello, I'm Mary Smith" will usually bring a friendly response from the other person. Or perhaps you sense that the other person feels he should know you and is not sure of your name. Don't play a guessing game with a coy "I'll bet you don't remember me." This puts him in an awkward position. Tell him your name and if you remember meeting him before, say so. "I'm Mary Smith—Mrs. Smith—and I think we met at the Jones home several months ago." On the other hand, if you are sure you should know the other person and can't remember his name, be frank to say, "I'm sorry. I can't think of your name although I'm sure we have met." This saves embarrassment in the long run. Trying the face-saving "How is it you spell your name?" might get the cool reply "S-m-i-t-h."

CORRECTING A WRONG INTRODUCTION

There are times when you are introduced to someone you have met before, perhaps several times, and that person doesn't remember you. It is best then just to acknowledge the introduction again rather than to embarrass him by emphasizing his lack of memory. If you are introduced incorrectly, let it go if it isn't too serious a mistake and you don't expect to see the other person again. However, if you have been mistakenly introduced as someone else who is also present in the group, or if this is a new neighbor whom you'll be seeing every day and your name was not given correctly, then correct it immediately: "I'm sorry, my name is such and such."

It's usually best to give the full name rather than to introduce or be introduced by a nickname. That can come later when those concerned are better acquainted. But for someone to be introduced as "Buffie" is not polite to either person unless it is a young child. Even then the courtesy of the right name should be given a child even though he may prefer to be called by the nickname.

INTRODUCING BY FIRST NAME

The question of when to use first names when meeting people or talking with them can sometimes be difficult to answer. This depends to a large extent on the degree of formality observed in the community where one lives. There is a growing tendency to use first names socially. However, it is best initially to introduce an older person by his last name: "This is

Mr. Older." A younger man may be introduced as "John Younger."

In our informal, relaxed day we laugh at the old custom of the wife calling her husband "Mr." even when speaking to him in private, personal conversation. But perhaps the pendulum tends to swing too far in the opposite direction. To call someone by his first name after the first casual introduction and without having been invited to do so, assumes a friendship that really doesn't exist. Younger people particularly should take care not to use an older person's first name in conversation unless they have been asked to do so. Trying to impress others by pretending a first-name friendship with an important person sometimes has a way of boomeranging. One should be careful not to use a person's first name in conversation with others unless he also uses it in direct conversation with that person. This habit of name-dropping is all too common in Christian circles and is at variance with the teaching of God's Word which warns against this sort of thing (James 2).

Parents sometimes attempt to build a spirit of camaraderie between themselves and their children by encouraging the use of first names. This often has the opposite effect and parents lose the respect which their children should give them and which the proper use of some form of "father" and "mother" helps to foster. Other family members such as aunts, uncles and grandparents may prefer a less formal title. "Grandfather" and "grandmother" are one thing (and they often like a shorter name), but "great-aunt" and "great-uncle" do make the person seem aged and a pet name might be preferred.

When introducing oneself, the usual form is "Mary Smith" or "John Smith" rather than using the titles of "Miss," "Mrs." or "Mr." Further identification may be given by saying, "I'm Johnny's mother" or "My husband has spoken of you many times," or something else that will identify you as married or single if that information is needed. In speaking to someone to whom "Mary Smith" means nothing, but "Mrs. John Smith" does, then make yourself clear. "I'm Mary Smith—Mrs. John Smith—and I am so happy to meet you." A man always introduces himself by his name without a title since it is obviously not necessary to call himself "Mr."

WIDOW'S CORRECT NAME

Many people seem not to understand that a widow always remains "Mrs. John Smith." She does not become "Mrs. Mary Smith" just because her husband is no longer living. There are times when a woman prefers to use another name for professional or business reasons, perhaps even using her maiden name, but socially she is always Mrs. John Smith.

Ordinarily "ma'am" and "sir" are heard only in certain parts of the country and even there they are not as commonly used. If they are used naturally, they have a very pleasing, respectful sound. Certainly it never hurts a young man to learn to say "sir" when speaking to an older man.

RECEIVING LINE INTRODUCTIONS

The rules for making introductions in a receiving line vary with the occasion. Generally the one standing first in line greets each arrival, shakes hands and introduces him to the next person and the process is repeated down the line. If the person first in line is not acquainted with the guests, each one will have to introduce himself. At a large reception, such as at a school, someone introduces each guest to the first one in line, who is usually the president.

TELEPHONE INTRODUCTIONS, MANNERS

There are also courteous ways of introducing oneself over the telephone. At home, the simplest answer to give when the phone rings is "Hello." Some people pick up the phone and say, "Yes?" But this is abrupt and gives the impression of impatience whether such is intended or not. Children are often trained to give the family name when answering: "This is the John Smith residence. Susie speaking"; and this is not incorrect. But since one has no way of knowing who is calling, it is safest to be as noncommittal as possible while at the same time being friendly, and a simple hello accomplishes this. Then the caller identifies himself in some way or asks to speak to a particular person and the conversation goes on from there.

The correct way to give one's name over the phone depends on the situation. Usually the titles of "Miss," "Mrs." and "Mr." are not used unless one is calling on business, and not always then. When talking to a stranger or handling business details, such as ordering something from a store, a woman uses "Miss Smith" or

"Mrs. Smith" (preferably with "John"). An older woman calling a much younger woman uses her title: "This is Mrs. Older" or "Miss Older." A younger person whether married or single gives her first name but uses the title of the older person. For example, "Hello, Mrs. Older. This is Mary Younger." A man calling a woman whom he knows well uses her first name; otherwise he calls her "Miss" or "Mrs." A young person calling a friend gives his name to whoever answers the phone just as he is used to being called, whether Jim, Sally or Janie.

There are certain telephone manners that are sometimes forgotten simply because we are not speaking face to face with the other person. There are times when a person dials a wrong number and then asks accusingly, "What number is this?" as though it were the other person's fault. One should not give his own number in such a situation, for he has no way of knowing who is asking or for what purpose. Instead, when asked such a question, one should answer, "What number are you dialing?" If it is a genuine call, the other person will give the number he wants and you can express regret and suggest that he dial again.

Sometimes people dial a number when they are not free to carry through a conversation without interruption. It is rude to place a call and then ask the person called to wait while you turn down the iron or put a snowsuit on a child or put a roast in the oven. If something comes up unexpectedly after the person has answered and it must be taken care of at once, explain the situation and ask if you may call back later. However, if the person who is called is just giving the baby a bath or leaving to catch a train, she should explain her situation and ask to call back. It is also rude to a guest to leave him sitting while you answer the phone and then carry on a lengthy conversation. Since he was there first, he has priority over interruptions.

CHILDREN USING THE PHONE

Young children should not be allowed to answer the phone indiscriminately. It is one thing to teach a child to answer correctly so that he can do so in an emergency. It is another to let a child answer the phone whenever it rings no matter who else is free to do so, and allow him to prattle away, perhaps hanging up without getting the one for whom the call was intended.

INVITATIONS BY PHONE

When giving an invitation by telephone, it really isn't polite to begin by asking, "What are you doing Saturday night?" It isn't only teenagers just beginning to date who begin an invitation this way; many adults do also. Instead, the invitation should be given first: "We'd like you and your husband to come to dinner Friday evening." Then, if the person invited does not want to come or cannot, she is able to decline without already having said the evening was free.

PAYING FOR PHONE CALLS

There is a discourteous telephone habit practiced by guests who seem to feel that the host's phone is theirs also. They feel free to make long-distance phone calls and think they will insult the host's hospitality if they offer to pay for the calls. This is a good way to insure not being asked back for a visit. No matter how rich the host may be or whether he is a close relative, if you make a long-distance call, ask the operator for the charges and leave the money—including the tax. If the host refuses to accept it, at least you have not presumed on his hospitality.

"As ye would that men should do to you, do ye also to them likewise" is a good rule to apply here as well as in the whole area of introductions.

3

CONVERSATION

"So likewise ye, except ye utter by the tongue words easy to be understood, how shall it be known what is spoken? For ye shall speak into the air." These words from I Corinthians 14 remind us to speak so that others will not only hear but clearly understand. Next to personal appearance, we are most often judged by how we speak and what we say. Here again there are simple rules governing conversation that keep it an art which can be mastered by anyone.

IMPROVING CONVERSATIONAL ABILITY

A good relationship with other people is made up of a composite of factors. Speech is one of the most important of these because it is the one we use most often to communicate with others. Conversation doesn't come with equal ease to everyone. But the person who really wants to be a better conversationalist can be. Although everyone may not learn to be an artist using colors, everyone can learn to paint pictures with words because the tools—accurate grammar, a wide vocabulary and correct pronunciation—are available to anyone who wants to acquire them.

PRONUNCIATION

Naturally one may mispronounce words or even use them incorrectly and still be understood. But since words are the basis of our communication with others, we should use them as accurately as possible. Speaking ability can be improved by listening to the way others speak, making use of the dictionary to increase word knowledge, and reading widely to gain information on a variety of subjects. Abraham Lincoln will forever be an example of one who learned through his own efforts to speak so that his words still have power to stir those who read them in cold print. In addition, the Christian has the advantage of being able to go for help to the source of wisdom and knowledge, God Himself. In Isaiah 50:4 the prophet said, "The LORD God hath given me the tongue of the learned, that I should know how to speak a word in season to him that is weary."

Whether we think of conversation as the words exchanged casually between neighbors over the back fence or those expressed formally in a panel discussion, there are principles we can learn which will help us speak more effectively. One is to pronounce and use words accurately, remembering that this will vary from one part of the country to another. How a word is pronounced and used in the South will be different from the way it is done in New England. In some parts of the South you are "carried" out to lunch; in the North, you are "taken." When moving permanently to another part of the country, it is probably best to adapt as much as possible to the speech patterns of the area. Ideally, we should try to weed out pronunciations that stamp us as being from a certain section, but this is difficult to do.

Sometimes we mispronounce words because we are not familiar with them. Words like *suite* (swēt), *chaise longue* (shāz lông) and *faux pas* (fō pä) should be checked in a dictionary. It's better not to use such words at all than to do so incorrectly.

MISUSING WORDS

There are other words and expressions that we sometimes misuse, and this stamps us as being somewhat ignorant. It's true, of course, that meanings of words often change from one decade to another. Such words as "cool" and "square" and "neat" do not have the same connotation today that they did some years ago. But there are other words which have not changed in meaning and yet have often been used incorrectly. A "house" is a building; "home" is the atmosphere and spirit of the place. We go home to a house; we pay the mortgage on the house, not on the home. "Folks" should not be used to refer to one's family. The abrupt "Pardon," although not strictly correct, is widely used. However "I beg your pardon" is more gracious. The words "woman" and "man" are quite all right for general use, while "lady" and "gentleman" are more correctly used to refer to the good manners of a person rather than to the individual. For example, "gentlemen" remove their hats in the house but "men" walk down the street.

INCREASING VOCABULARY

Another way to improve conversational ability is to

have an adequate vocabulary. The English language is rich and varied, although it isn't thought of in that way because we so seldom use all the words at our disposal. For instance, we use the word "wonderful" to mean unusual, great, magnificent, beautiful, charming, accomplished, delightful, spectacular, daring, delicious, and so on. Each of these words if used would convey a much more precise meaning than the general term "wonderful" ever could. We are like the man who found the dictionary difficult to read "because it kept changing the subject all the time." Nevertheless we could enrich our vocabulary and improve our communication with others if we used it more often.

USING FAMILIAR WORDS

Of course, having a large vocabulary does not necessarily mean knowing and using a lot of big words. Often we use a many-syllabled word when a short one would be just as effective or more so. The use of a common word makes us more easily understood. But whether a word is long or short it ought to be familiar to those with whom we are talking.

There seems to be an increasing tendency to avoid the obvious word and to use instead a less direct one, and so our speech becomes fuzzy instead of being sharp and precise. We don't "start" something, but "instigate" or "inaugurate" it. We don't "use" an object, but "utilize" it. We don't just "get" something; it must be "obtained" or "secured." It isn't enough simply to "talk" with someone; we must "dialogue" or "communicate."

Each of these words has its place but is not necessarily always clearer or more accurate than the shorter, more common word. Often such specialized vocabulary, or jargon, obscures the meaning instead of making it clearer. A specialized vocabulary is needed in certain professions which require specific terms to convey a precise meaning. These expressions have a proper place, but not when used constantly in ordinary conversation. Using jargon of any kind when not speaking professionally is discourteous to the listener who is not familiar with it.

Still another principle to follow in conversation is to fit the words to the group we talk to. Unless we do this, we will never get our ideas across, no matter how many words we know or how well we use them. The value of this principle is evident in the communication gap between adults and adolescents, which is often due to a difference in the meaning of the words each uses. This is where we see the wisdom of using common, ordinary words in conversation. Most adults can't hope to keep up with teenage vocabulary because what is in today may be out next week. But an adult may still reach teenagers, whether speaking to them as a group or privately, if he uses words that are familiar to him and them.

It is equally incorrect for young people to exclusively use their specialized vocabulary when talking to adults. Unfortunately, those who work with young people too often speak to an adult audience as they would to a teenage group instead of adapting to the adult level of experience and vocabulary.

SLANG

This gap is bridged to a certain extent by the slang all of us use in our speech. Slang adds spice to a language, and it is not offensive if it is used at the proper time and place. But slang which is right for teenagers would not be acceptable at an afternoon tea party for elderly ladies even though there were nothing wrong with the actual words. For example, a teenage girl may call a group of her friends "you guys," and be understood by them. But it would be in poor taste for her to speak to a group of her mother's friends in this way. This is an instance of suiting the words to the group.

Everyone at some time makes a mistake in speaking, usually when it is too late to do anything about it. The only thing to do is to let it go without making too much of it, and then resolve not to make the same mistake again.

ACCEPTING COMPLIMENTS

There is another area in which we often show a lack of manners without intending to. It is when someone pays us a compliment and we do not know how to accept it. We are often embarrassed and try to explain away or at least deprecate our ability, the new dress, the job promotion or whatever it might be. All that is necessary in reply to a compliment is a simple and sincere thank you.

HANDLING PERSONAL QUESTIONS

Sometimes people make the mistake of asking personal questions which we don't want to answer. "Do you like to golf?" is a personal question, but it is quite different from "How much did you pay for your dress?" There may be a time when these questions are asked purposely and one instinctively wants to give an insulting answer in return. Don't. Usually such questions are asked thoughtlessly with no offense intended.

Just remember that no one ever needs to give information he does not wish to give. It may be that you don't mind telling the price of the dress because it was such a fantastic bargain that you feel quite elated over it. But if you don't want to tell, just say, "I'm sorry, I'd rather not say," and do it as politely as possible. If your voice is calm and pleasant, the answer will not sound rude.

ARGUMENTS

In any conversation a really polite person does not argue, no matter how offensive another person might be in the dogmatic statements he makes. Nor is he offensively dogmatic in return. This is one time when it is most obvious whether good manners are ingrained or are just a thin veneer. A Christian particularly should guard against this so that his conversation is "always with grace, seasoned with salt, that ye may know how ye ought to answer every man" (Colossians 4:6). No matter how deeply you feel on a subject, don't allow yourself to become rude and discourteous just because someone else is. The safest rule for everyone to follow is to think twice before speaking. If this were done, it might eliminate some of the rude statements, the cutting comments, the boring stories, the gossip and the unkind remarks that make up so large a part of the average conversation.

The Christian has a particular responsibility to be effective when talking with others because this is one way in which he can very naturally witness to his faith in Christ. Very few of us will ever win friends and influence people in large groups, but we can do so in informal conversation with neighbors in the backyard, over coffee at a PTA meeting, or with guests who are visiting us. This is the place to practice the ability to state opinions, share ideas and use words effectively.

TAKING PART IN CONVERSATION

Conversation is like a game of ping-pong with the ball going back and forth among those in the group, not in idle talk but in an exchange of ideas and opinions both humorous and serious. There must be give and take, and this puts a responsibility on each person. While it is impolite for one person to dominate the conversation, it is also impolite for someone merely to sit and listen without contributing. Such an attitude says in effect, "I don't care enough about the rest of you to bother talking." Of course this isn't usually true, because many naturally quiet people find it difficult to converse in a group, while others are timid about expressing their ideas. But if each of us remembers that good manners mean consideration for others, we will make an effort to carry our share of the conversational burden and so influence others by our opinions. In good conversation, one listens politely and then in turn one contributes politely.

One of the best ways to get a reputation as a good

conversationalist is to be interested in the other person. It isn't so much what *we* say, but what we encourage the other person to say that makes us remembered as interesting people to talk to.

Talking with a friend is a fairly simple matter, for there is a basis of mutual interests with which to begin. We are neighbors, or attend the same church, or work in the same office, or have children in the same school. All of this provides material for conversation. If the friend is someone "of like precious faith," we should also find it very easy to talk about the Lord Jesus Christ as One who is so much an integral part of our daily lives that He is a natural part of our conversations. Often this is not true, and we lose out on opportunities to strengthen each other in the faith because other topics—the weather, our work, our children—come more readily to our lips.

It's more difficult to begin and carry on a conversation with people we don't know. Yet this is where good manners show: "I'm Mary Smith from down the block and we're glad to have you in our neighborhood" or office or school or club. It isn't so much the words that are spoken in this initial encounter, but the warmth and sincerity with which they are said that will encourage the other person to respond.

WITNESSING

A friendly conversational time like this may be the only opportunity many of us have to witness. Since witnessing is really just telling someone about something we know, ordinary conversation is one of the most natural times to do it. This does not mean that

we start right in by buttonholing the person and argu-
ing with him. One of the arts of conversation is interest in the other person, and so a simple question
about where he goes to church is a natural one to ask.
If he names one, you can probe a bit further by telling
where you go and giving a brief warm word of your
love for the Lord. If he does not attend church, you
are at liberty to invite him to yours. Perhaps this is all
the witnessing you do this one time, but you have
carried on the conversational game properly and have
shown a friendly interest which could have eternal
results.

Because ease in conversation depends so much on
individual personality, no rule can be made about
when one should talk to others. One person is not
necessarily friendlier than another just because he
talks easily to the clerk at the check-out counter, or
the cab driver, or the person in the seat next to him. It
is just that the one finds it easier to express himself in
words. However, most of us need to learn to express
our interest in others, and this is why we must ask for
wisdom to know when to speak the "word in season"
which might help someone.

We must remember that the principle of doing "the
kindest thing in the kindest way" means avoiding controversial subjects which may turn into unpleasant
arguments. In private conversation each person must
take the responsibility for this on his own shoulders. In
a social gathering, the host or hostess must steer guests
away from such topics, and this requires more tact and
wisdom than most of us have.

CONTROVERSIAL SUBJECTS

What is a controversial subject? One type is the dirty joke or the off-color story which ought to be automatically taboo in any group. Yet almost everyone is exposed to this at some time. The way in which this is handled is important because we are talking about good manners, which mean being polite and kind to others regardless of their behavior. This is not always easy to do. One can consistently not laugh at such jokes and stories. In an office, or in any group, you will soon spot the one who tells them and can try to avoid him as much as possible. You may have to tell a person frankly that you don't care to hear this kind of thing. This needn't be done in a holier-than-thou tone but in a friendly manner: "I don't care for that story, but have you heard this one?" Then tell one that isn't offensive.

Politics is a subject which traditionally has been considered controversial. Of course it's foolish to steer all talk away from politics just before an election in which everyone is deeply concerned. But to allow a political discussion, either at a social gathering or in private conversation, to go on to the point of shouting and name-calling is also foolish.

Religion is another subject that etiquette books agree should be left out of conversations. And it should be if it involves a bitter argument over church policies and personalities. But if, as has already been said, talking about religion means sharing one's personal faith, then it has a proper place. Every Christian should be like the early apostles who said, "We cannot

but speak the things which we have seen and heard"
(Acts 4:20).

But in this conversational witness we must remember that there are other factors which affect the words of a testimony. Our personal appearance, our manners at the dinner table, our treatment of a waiter in the restaurant speak volumes to the observer. Any rude or tactless or dogmatic statements we make on other subjects fix a certain impression in the minds of those around us. Then when we speak of Christian love, the words do not match our actions. The words may be intended as a witness for the Lord but the effect is to turn people from Him.

All the skill and tact and winsomeness and graciousness and intelligence and knowledge a Christian has, should be used always if he is to be an ambassador for Christ in his conversation with others.

4

CORRESPONDENCE

Nowhere is the value of letter writing more clearly seen than in the letters of Paul in the New Testament. They were written from his heart to the hearts of the recipients and expressed love, concern, sympathy, rebuke, warning, instruction and gratitude. Though filled with deep doctrinal truths, the letters were written out of love for friends in Christ. If we would think of our letters in this way, we might find them easier to write.

LETTER WRITING SUPPLIES

Many people find letter writing a chore and so miss out on what could be an enjoyable and rewarding experience. There are ways we can make letter writing easier. One is to have on hand a supply of various kinds of paper as well as pens and stamps, and a definite place to keep them. Another is to know the basic principles of when, how and what to write.

For any kind of social letter, white paper of good texture with a matching envelope is always right. Sometimes men also like a cream or a gray paper, while women prefer the many delicate shades available in pale green, blue, tan or gray. Most stationery is boxed with matching envelopes which have attractive

65

linings, or envelopes may be bought separately. As a general rule women should avoid the use of "cute" notepaper, though this kind is suitable for young girls and teenagers.

It is well to have a supply of several kinds of stationery because of the variety of letters we must write. One general kind that is most often used is a single sheet (about 5×7 inches) which is folded in half to insert in the envelope. If one's name and address are printed or engraved at the top of the page, they may either be centered in three lines or written across the page in a single line. A married woman uses her married name, "Mrs. John Smith," but a single woman may use "Miss" or not, just as she prefers. If a monogram or initials are used, they are put at the upper left of the page. In ordering paper be sure to get a supply of plain sheets because only the first page of a letter should have the name and address.

Another kind of paper used less frequently than others is a heavy, white double sheet used in answering formal invitations. This is usually folded once and put in a matching envelope. However, plain white paper of good quality can be used just as well for this purpose.

INFORMALS

"Informals" in stationery refer to a folded notepaper about 3×4 inches with matching envelopes. These are used in answering informal invitations, dashing off a quick note to a friend, or writing notes of sympathy, congratulations or thanks. Many brides find it convenient to order a supply of informals when they order their wedding invitations. The name is engraved or printed on an informal in the center of the first page: "Miss Mary Louise Smith" or "Mrs. John Charles Smith." If the address is also given, it is put in the lower right corner usually in smaller type. An informal may also be used to give an invitation without having to write a note on the inside. Used this way, the invitation reads:

Dinner on Friday

June 23—6:30

Mrs. John Charles Smith

1100 Lake Shore Drive

RSVP

And the answer may be returned in the same way.

It is well to remember that it isn't necessary to spend a great deal of money on stationery. Even the ten-cent store has a wide choice available both in kind and quality which is very satisfactory. Simplicity is the key here as in most areas in life.

CALLING CARDS

In addition to the general kinds of stationery already mentioned, many people like to have a supply of calling cards though these are seldom used any longer for a formal call. These are fairly small, about 3½ × 2½ inches, and the name, written out with no abbreviations, is always engraved on them. They are used in the same way an informal is used and also may be enclosed in a gift. If such cards are mailed, they should be put in a larger envelope because of post-office regulations about the size of envelopes.

BUSINESS CARDS

There are also business cards which are used by both men and women. These are printed, and initials

United Products, Inc.

John C. Smith

and abbreviations may be used on them. The company name may appear in the middle of the card and in the lower left-hand corner is the person's name. Or the name is in the middle of the card, particularly if the man is an executive, and his title and company name are printed in the lower left:

```
┌─────────────────────────────────────┐
│                                       │
│                                       │
│                                       │
│                                       │
│            John C. Smith              │
│                                       │
│                                       │
│         President                     │
│      United Products, Inc.            │
│                                       │
└─────────────────────────────────────┘
```

A woman prints her name on a business card: "Miss Mary Louise Smith" or "Mrs. John C. Smith" or "Mary Smith Jones." If she is best known in business by her maiden name, she may keep it for business cards even after her marriage, though her married name is always used on social cards.

RULES FOR LETTER WRITING

Regardless of all else, there are certain basic requirements every letter or note should meet. The writing must be legible and the words spelled correctly.

The person who really has trouble writing legibly may correctly use a typewriter for almost all social letters, though he should type on one side of the sheet only. However, everyone should learn to write clearly because there are certain kinds of letters which must always be handwritten. These are letters of sympathy, thank you notes, formal invitations which are not engraved, and the replies to such invitations. Since these are always brief, they should not be too much of a problem for anyone to write.

In writing any letter one should suit the paper and the color of ink used to the person and the occasion. A flamboyant person might write a letter of congratulations to a friend in red ink on violet-colored paper, but to write a letter of condolence in the same way would be in poor taste.

The mechanics of letter writing follow definite rules. If the address is not printed or engraved on the stationery, it should be written in the upper right-hand corner of the first page with the date just below it. On a shorter note one may put the address or even just the date at the far left of the paper just below the signature level. It isn't necessary to include the address when one is writing to close friends or relatives who already know it, but the date should always be included.

The order in which one writes the pages varies with individual preference. If single sheets are used, one may write either on one side only or on both sides if the paper is not too thin. If folded notepaper is used, the pages could be written in order, one through four, or one may write pages one and four and then open the paper flat and write across pages two and three. If you know you'll only be writing two pages, it looks nicer to write on pages one and three. No matter what order is followed, the pages should be numbered for the convenience of the one receiving the letter.

SOCIAL LETTERS

The heading of a social letter is informal: "Dear Mary," "Dear Grandma," "Dear Children," and so on. The degree of intimacy depends on the depth of feeling between the writer and the receiver. It is usually best to be somewhat restrained in expressing sentiments in letters because years may change the feelings, and letters have sometimes been used against the writer with damaging results.

The body of the letter should be spaced so that the page will look neat. If the letter is to be short, begin far enough down that it will not all be above the middle of the page.

One of the reasons we sometimes put off writing letters is that we don't know what to say. Actually, we should write as though we were talking to the person. Usually our conversation with a friend is not stilted. We use abbreviations, we express amazement, we show sympathy, we joke. Carry this over into letter writing so that the letter sounds like you. Instead of:

Dear Aunt Mary,

I take my pen in hand to express my deep gratitude to you for your thoughtfulness in procuring the necessary place settings to complete my twelve-piece china service . . .

try:

Dear Aunt Mary,

You're a darling to finish getting our china for us! Now we can have the whole family to dinner at once and nobody will have to use plastic dishes. How did you ever know that this is what we wanted for an anniversary present more than anything else?

Even the most staid and correct Aunt Mary would appreciate the second note more than the first.

The closing of a social letter ranges through "Sincerely," "Sincerely yours," "Cordially," "Affectionately," "With love," "Lovingly," and so on. To end a letter with "Hastily" or "In haste" seems rather rude. Even if we did have to snatch time from something important to dash off a note, it isn't necessary to let the other person know that he got only the fringes of our time.

EXPRESSIONS LIKE "IN CHRIST"

Often Christians feel that every letter should end with some form of "In Christ," or "Your friend in Christ." This is a very individual matter. It is certainly appropriate when writing to a personal friend and when the letter is a warm, heartfelt expression of friendship. It is true that the letters in the New Testament often end with a prayer for God's blessing on those to whom the letter was written. But this could be a case of casting "pearls before swine" if the expression means nothing to the person receiving the letter. Such an ending would not be appropriate on the average business letter. Of course, if you honestly feel that such an expression would arouse interest in the one receiving the letter and you are in a position to follow up in a personal way, you should use your own judgment in the matter.

SIGNATURE

The signature, always handwritten, also depends to some extent on the relationship of the persons. A man does not use his title, but signs simply "John Smith," or to friends, "John." A married woman writing to friends signs her name "Mary"; to acquaintances, "Mary Smith"; to strangers or on business, "Mary Smith," and in parentheses below, "Mrs. John Smith." This last is not necessary, of course, if her name is printed at the top of the page.

Whenever a woman types a letter, whether it is for business or social reasons, she writes her signature "Mary Smith," and below it types "Mrs. John Smith," which may be enclosed in parentheses. It is not correct to write one's name as "Mrs." except when signing a hotel register. If you must write a note asking that the milk delivery be stopped for a time, either "Mrs. Smith," "Mary Smith" or even just your initials may be used. Letters should not be addressed to "Mrs. Mary Smith" since a woman always correctly uses her husband's name even if she is a widow. Her name is best listed in that way in the phone book as a protection against unscrupulous people.

USE OF "JUNIOR," "SENIOR," II, III

There is sometimes confusion about the use of "Junior" or the numerals II or III used with a name. "Junior" means that the man's father is still living. It is part of his name and is used by his wife and written "Mrs. John Smith, Jr." A capital *J* is used when the word is abbreviated and a small one when it is written out. It is not correct for a man to call himself "Sr." This is only used to differentiate between a widow and a daughter-in-law, and then only to avoid confusing the two names.

When II follows a name, it indicates that the man has an older living relative of the same name, an uncle perhaps, but not his father. A grandfather would be John Smith; the father is John Smith, Jr.; the son is John Smith III. When the grandfather dies, the father becomes John Smith and the son, John Smith, Jr.

THE ENVELOPE

The envelope of a letter is important because it represents the person writing. A wrinkled envelope with a stamp that is stuck on crooked, the ink blotted and the address barely legible may be pardoned when it comes from one who is loved for qualities other than neatness. Too often such an envelope marks the writer as a very careless person. A letter after all is an expression of oneself and even the envelope should make the best impression possible. It should always carry a return address in the upper left-hand corner (the position preferred by the post office) or on the back flap, and should include the zip code. The address may be written in step style—each line indented several spaces, or in block style—a straight margin on the left, with no punctuation at the end of the lines.

The correct title of a person should always be put on the envelope and the name should not stand alone. Men and women are always addressed as "Mrs.," "Mr.," "Dr." or "Miss." Letters to girls are addressed "Miss" regardless of age. Boys under ten may be addressed as "Master," and then no title is used until they are eighteen when, of course, they are always "Mr."

It really isn't correct or polite to write "Personal" on mail which is sent to someone at his home. It is all right to do so on confidential mail sent to a business office where a secretary or a central letter opening service handles the mail. If a friend delivers a note to someone, the envelope is left unsealed and on the front is written:

Mrs. Richard Jones

Kindness of Mary Smith

THANK YOU NOTES

Among the various kinds of social letters are those which absolutely must be written whether we want to write them or not. One of these is the thank you note. This is written for three specific reasons: for a gift, for overnight hospitality, for some particular courtesy one has received. There may be other reasons for writing thank you notes, of course. In some places a note is expected after one has been a dinner guest even though thanks have been said orally.

Thank you notes must be written promptly, sincerely, specifically and by hand. They do not receive an answer because they are an expression of appreciation for a courtesy the other person has already given. One should acknowledge a birthday gift within a week, a Christmas gift within two weeks, and a wedding gift within three weeks. This time limit may have to be modified to some extent, of course, particularly if a great many wedding gifts arrive at one time. But setting a time limit for oneself is a wise precaution. A note of thanks for hospitality should be written within two or three days of a visit and certainly no later than a week. It may be written on an informal or on a single sheet of paper since only a few lines are expected. This doesn't have to be a chatty, lengthy letter; it is written for a specific reason.

In thanking for a gift, be sincere but not gushy, and mention the gift in some way. For example:

Dear Aunt Harriet,

John and I are delighted with the gift of silver. I'm sure you spent hours looking for a tray that matched our set so perfectly. Knowing you looked for it during your lunch hour makes us appreciate it even more.

Please come and have supper with us some Sunday evening soon.

Lovingly,

Mary

The sincerity of a bread and butter letter which says, "Thank you so much for the wonderful weekend away from the hot city," though brief, is appreciated by a hostess even though you thanked her in person.

Perhaps you visited a friend for a day and she spent the afternoon driving you around town; or a neighbor took care of your children in an emergency; or someone put up a friend for you overnight because you did not have room. All of these kindnesses deserve a thank you note in return.

LETTERS OF CONGRATULATION

Then there are letters of congratulation which are written any time one hears something nice about a friend or business acquaintance. It may be news of an engagement, a wedding, a graduation, a job promotion, a new baby, or any success, achievement or recognition which comes to someone you know. These letters may be formal or informal, handwritten or typed. The elements they must have are warmth and sincerity, and the evidence that the person writing is really rejoicing over the good news. This is a scriptural principle, for we are told to rejoice with those that rejoice. The one receiving a congratulatory letter should acknowledge it with a brief note of thanks.

LETTERS OF CONDOLENCE

A letter of condolence is difficult to write because of the inadequacy of words to express sympathy. Because of the personal nature of such a letter, it is impossible to set a rule as to what should be said. A note of sympathy over the death of an aged grandparent who has been an invalid for twenty years will be different from that to a young wife at the sudden loss of her husband in an auto accident. But whatever is written, it should be brief, sincere and comforting. If the people who are bereaved are not Christians, this is no time to preach at them; if they are, it is not a time to write a theological treatise on the mysteries of God's will. Just be sympathetic and comforting, remembering that the best comfort is an appropriate verse of Scripture which God will fit to the situation.

Letters of sympathy are usually handwritten on good stationery, not on casual, informal notepaper. If you use a sympathy card, be sure to write a few personal lines expressing your feelings rather than just signing your name. A letter of condolence to a family from a business firm about a business associate is usually dictated and typed. These letters should usually be answered within six weeks or as soon as the one receiving them feels able to do so.

LETTERS NOT TO WRITE

There are certain social letters which ought not to be written. An angry note dropped in the mailbox goes its irretrievable way, usually leaving the writer regretting his hasty act. Sometimes you intend a note to be just a neighborly word of advice but the other person may not interpret it that way. For example:

Dear Neighbor,

I'm sure you will want to repay us for the two dozen tulip bulbs your children dug out of our garden yesterday. We would appreciate your keeping them out of our yard in the future.

The neighbors will not accept this as a friendly note, especially if they know it was the children down the block who dug up the flowers.

INVITATIONS—FORMAL, INFORMAL

Correspondence also includes writing and replying to a variety of invitations. Most of these follow a prescribed pattern which, when learned, is not difficult to remember. The most rigid traditional rules apply to wedding invitations and announcements which are discussed in a later chapter (see Weddings). The basic rule to remember is that invitations are replied to in the same degree of formality in which they are given.

Formal invitations are easily recognized because they are always worded in the third person. These are always engraved or handwritten on plain, good quality stationery of a white, cream or ivory color. Formal invitations are sent for weddings, wedding receptions, formal dinners, official dinners and luncheons. Whether it is an invitation to a concert, a dinner, a luncheon, a tea, or to meet an honored guest, and whether sent by an individual or by an organization, a completely engraved invitation reads:

Mr. and Mrs. John Smith
request the pleasure of your company
at dinner
on Monday, the first of January
at seven o'clock
1100 Summit Road

RSVP

with, of course, the proper change in wording to fit the occasion. If the invitation is handwritten, the wording and spacing follow the engraved example. Sometimes a partially engraved invitation is sent with the name of the guest, the date and the time filled in by hand.

The answer to the formal invitation is given in the same way:

Mr. and Mrs. Richard Jones
accept with pleasure
the kind invitation of
Mr. and Mrs. Smith
for dinner
on Monday, January the first
at seven o'clock

If one is unable to attend, the regret is written in exactly the same way except that the day and hour need not be mentioned. It is repeated in an acceptance to be sure there is no misunderstanding of either. When one must decline an invitation, it is well to give a reason, such as previous plans, unexpected company, illness in the family, and so on.

This may seem very stiff and formal to you and perhaps no one in your community ever answers an invitation this way so that you would feel foolish doing so. You will have to use your own judgment in this. The main point, of course, is to reply. It's better to answer a formal invitation by an informal reply than not to answer at all. However, this is properly the rule to observe and it is well to know it because in other communities you might be criticized for not following it. Most invitations these days are informal, but if one comes formally, answer it that way.

Most of us more frequently send and receive informal invitations. These may be written on an informal, on a visiting card, on a single sheet of paper, on a clever original cutout such as a heart-shaped invitation for a valentine party, or in any other way one wishes. It isn't the stationery used but the wording of the invitation that distinguishes the formal from the informal. The informal invitation is written in the second person by the wife for herself and her husband and it is answered in the same way. For example:

Dear Sally,

    Will you and Bill be able to go with us to the college concert on Friday? We'll pick you up at seven-thirty.

    We have extra tickets and would love to have your company for the evening.

                     Sincerely,
                      Mary

If they are mutual friends, the answer would be, "Dear Mary, Bill and I are delighted to accept your invitation for the concert on Friday. Seven-thirty will be convenient." If it is an older couple inviting a younger couple, the answer would be, "Dear Mrs. Smith," etc.

TELEPHONE INVITATION

An invitation by telephone is quick and direct. "Are you and your husband free to have dinner with us on Saturday?" If the wife knows the evening is free, she answers immediately, "Yes, thank you, we'd love to come." If she knows it isn't, she gives an immediate "No, I'm sorry." Sometimes she will have to check her husband's schedule, and agrees to call back as soon as possible. Such telephone invitations are given for dinner, lunch, a picnic, a buffet supper or a concert—any time when an informal written invitation is appropriate.

A hostess may follow a telephoned invitation with a note of reminder, but this certainly is not necessary. It's the responsibility of the one receiving the invitation to remember the date and time. If a written reminder is sent, it could be just "We are looking forward to your having dinner with us this coming Saturday at six." No answer to this reminder is expected.

BUSINESS INVITATION

Business invitations follow the general rules for social invitations with the necessary adjustment in wording:

Mr. John Smith
President of United Products
requests the pleasure of your company
[etc.]

These invitations are sent to people by the names by which they are known professionally. This means "Mrs. John Charles Smith" is addressed as "Mrs. Mary Louise Smith" even though this would be incorrect socially.

RSVP

Any invitation with an RSVP in the corner must be answered. If no reply is requested, either the hostess is sure you will be coming or else whether you do or not will make no difference in her plans. This is true, for example, of a large afternoon tea or an open house where people come and go over a period of time and enough refreshments are planned to take care of everyone.

RSVP is the abbreviation of the French *Répondez s'il vous plaît* (please answer) and should be written with no periods, either all capital letters or a capital *R* and the rest small letters. Sometimes "Please reply" is used, but RSVP is more common. If one wants a reply only from those who cannot come, one puts "Regrets only" under the RSVP.

Organizations frequently include answer cards with invitations to dinners, which provide a place to check whether or not one is coming. This simplifies the responsibility for the one invited, who should return the card promptly. It is inconsiderate to assume that the organization will know you are not coming if you do not return the card. Actually, no RSVP would be necessary on any invitation if people were thoughtful enough to answer each one as a matter of courtesy.

BUSINESS LETTER

Another type of correspondence is the business letter. A firm should not try to economize on the stationery it uses in the competitive business world. The stationery should be plain but of good quality with the letterhead designed by someone who knows his business. The preferred paper size is $8\frac{1}{2} \times 11$ inches because, when folded properly, it fits either of the two standard-size business envelopes, and also because that size stationery fits into a file without slipping to the bottom.

One of the chief requirements of a business letter is that it be brief and direct. The idea that a long business letter is more friendly than a short one is wrong. If the business can be settled in one sentence, so much the better, although a second paragraph of "Thank you for your help" or "Thank you for looking into this matter" conveys friendly courtesy. The lack of any indication of graciousness is noticed and makes a bad impression. Such a lack is not only poor manners, it is also poor business practice.

CORRECT FORM

The properly written business letter follows a definite form. If the address of the company is not printed somewhere on the stationery, it should be enclosed in the letter at the upper left of the paper with the date just below it. (It is also correct to place these items to the right of the page although the preferred style nowadays is flush left.) It is better not to write numerals for the date, 7/1/69, but to write out the month, July 1, 1969, because this is clear at a glance.

On the left side of the paper, four spaces below the level of the date, are the name, address and city of the person(s) addressed. These are single-spaced. Two spaces below is the salutation, which is followed by a colon. Separate the body of the letter from the salutation by two spaces and leave the same number of spaces between the body of the letter and the closing. The words used in closing should fit the formality of the letter, although "Sincerely" or "Yours truly" is always correct. If a signature is typed on the letter, four spaces should be left between the closing phrase and it in order to have room also for a handwritten signature.

Business letters are usually single-spaced with double spacing between paragraphs. The style may either be step or block but it should be consistent throughout the letter. The block style is favored by most typists as it allows greater speed and gives a neat, clean-cut appearance. The sentences should be short, directly worded and properly spaced on the page depending on the length of the letter. The type should be clean and sharp so that the letter has a neat appearance.

AVOIDING CLICHES

Old clichés from a past generation such as "per our agreement," and "yours of the 15th inst. at hand" or "beg to state" are never used. Try not to say, "Enclosed please find" when "We enclose" or "Enclosed is" is more direct. Use "because" instead of "owing to the fact that," and "soon" rather than "at an early date." All the wordiness should be eliminated but not the friendliness.

Whether the business letter is long and fairly technical as some must be, or short and dealing with one item, it follows this style:

Street address
City
Date (written out)

Name of person
Business
Address
City, state, zip

Dear Sir:

The estimate you have made for landscaping our lawn and garden is satisfactory. You may proceed with the work in May as you have suggested.

Thank you for telling us about the saving we will have by your doing the work now.

Yours truly,

Mary Smith

(Mrs. John Smith)

When you write to a business firm but you want a certain person to take care of the matter, the company name comes first in the heading and the name of the individual is put under the city and state and is written "Attention Mr. F. C. Smith." The same words may be put at the lower left of the envelope when addressing a business firm but requiring the attention of a specific individual.

Every letter, regardless of the kind or purpose, should be written courteously. Even a letter of complaint to a store should not be offensive in tone, especially since the one receiving it very likely did not make the mistake in the first place.

Each of us should remember that the command to keep our speech "always seasoned with grace" applies to the written as well as the spoken word.

5

TABLE SETTING AND SERVING

Most of us need a frequent reminder of the words in Luke 12:15 that "a man's life consisteth not in the abundance of the things which he possesseth." Material possessions are not the most important part of life. Yet things are necessary for our daily living, and we should know how to make the best use of them and at the same time keep them in the proper perspective.

TABLE LINENS AND DISHES

There was a time when a girl began to accumulate her linen and silver long before she had any prospects of marriage. It is not as necessary today to begin married life with a quantity of household linens, nor does the average homemaker need as many towels and tablecloths as formerly. Automatic equipment and the many new materials make laundering so much easier that we can run a house with a smaller supply of linens.

In fact, the type of table linens and dishes used depends on many variables, including personal taste, the size of the family, the size of one's house, how much entertaining one does, the amount of money one can spend, and many other factors. The hostess in the tiny apartment who must serve on a small table which has to double as a dining table, a desk and an end table, probably doesn't even have a large damask tablecloth with matching napkins. On the other hand, even the hostess in a large home who entertains frequently often prefers lace, linen or cotton tablecloths, or place mats which fit a variety of occasions.

It is wise to buy the best table furnishings that one can afford rather than to buy a cheap imitation. A good quality cotton tablecloth is better than a cheap lace cloth. It's also wise to remember that the extreme or overly ornate in anything soon goes out of style, while simplicity never does. This is as true in silver and china as in dresses and hats.

We should choose table furnishings in terms of their value to us personally and not according to what some book says is proper. We need to consider the appropriateness of an item—whether it will fit our pattern of living; its durability—if it is so fragile that it can only be used on special occasions, it is likely not worth the money; its practicality—do we want it enough to go without something else we might use more? All of these are matters to consider in buying china, silver and glassware.

Not many young couples can afford to start out with a twelve-piece place setting of everything, and the question arises as to the most practical plan to follow in selecting silverware and china. Should they choose a sterling silver pattern, bone china and the finest crystal, trusting they will be given some pieces as gifts and acquire others through the years? Or should they begin with silverplate and less expensive china and glassware? This is entirely an individual matter dependent on some of the factors mentioned earlier.

SILVERWARE

One couple going to a remote, primitive mission field would find sterling silver a foolish investment; another in the same circumstances would want this touch of elegance to offset their primitive living conditions. A couple in one place might find eyebrows raised enviously if they were able to set a table for twelve with sterling, while in another place they would be criticized if they had only stainless steel. Each one must decide for himself what fits best in his own circumstances.

We often speak of china, silver and linen when actually we are using earthenware, stainless steel and cotton. Each of these has its proper place and usefulness, but we should know what we mean by the words.

The general term silverware is used to refer to sterling, silver plate or stainless steel. Sterling is the same metal throughout the piece so that there is nothing to wear away. This means that it will last forever. Sterling really grows more beautiful with constant use because any scratches blend together on the surface and enhance the appearance of the silver. It is constant use that keeps sterling from needing polishing, for tarnishing comes from disuse.

Plated silver, which is metal covered with silver, lasts a long time although eventually it may need to be replated. It is less expensive than sterling and there are many lovely patterns to choose from.

A good set of stainless steel sometimes costs almost as much as plate though there are also very inexpensive sets. Stainless steel is good looking, durable, and requires no care. We usually think that stainless steel is appropriate only for everyday family use; but there is no reason for anyone to be ashamed if that is all one can afford, and to never entertain just because one has neither sterling nor plated silver.

Two other metals used for silverware, though not as often, are Dirilyte, which is a gold color and is the same metal throughout the piece, and pewter, which retains its rich color and shine without requiring polishing.

BASIC PLACE SETTING

The minimum place setting of any of these is a dinner knife, a dinner fork, a teaspoon, a salad fork, a dessert spoon which is also used for soup or cereal, and an individual butter spreader. A complete place setting would add to the above a dessert knife and fork, a fish fork, a bouillon spoon, an iced tea spoon and a fruit knife. The importance of any of these depends on how much they will be used. One should always specify just what one wants included in a place setting, since some people prefer to have an extra teaspoon rather than a butter spreader. One should never hesitate to ask advice from the store when buying any of these table furnishings.

CHINA

Many people do not own a set of real china dishes, for they are fairly expensive. China refers to hard, translucent porcelain. It is not moisture-absorbent even when it is cracked, and a chipped place will not discolor from exposure. Because fine china is hard, it doesn't break easily. When a fine china dish is held to the light, one can see the shadow of one's fingers through it.

Pottery and earthenware, on the other hand, are more porous and can't stand intense heat. Earthenware is opaque rather than translucent. It is more easily chipped than fine china, although there are varying degrees of hardness in earthenware.

We are all familiar also with melamine or plastic dishes which are soft and easily affected by heat. They are extremely durable since they will not break easily, though they do discolor and need frequent cleaning with baking soda or a commercial preparation. They come in a variety of patterns and prices. Each of these three has its proper place in the average home.

In addition there is a variety of informal china, a very loose term used to include glass salad plates, wooden salad bowls and cheese trays, and serving dishes of silver, brass and pewter. One may have a variety of such dishes because they are relatively inexpensive.

The kind and amount of china one buys depend to a large extent on the entertaining one does, the amount of storage space in the house, and the cost of replacing items that will inevitably be broken. In this connection it is wise to buy open stock whenever possible. This means that the pattern is one the store will carry for a reasonable number of years and that one may buy individual pieces rather than an entire set at a time.

BASIC PLACE SETTING

A five-piece place setting of china usually includes a dinner plate, a bread and butter plate, a salad plate, a cup and a saucer.

GLASSWARE

The kind of glassware one buys is determined by the same principles of usefulness and practicality. It's fun to have at least a minimum of crystal which sparkles and has a bell-like ring when tapped, but this kind is very fragile. So most people depend on the more serviceable glassware which still can be attractive. Even the ten-cent store has a variety of glassware either in stemmed goblets or straight-sided glasses, colored or plain, which make an attractive table appearance and yet may be washed by the junior members of the family.

TABLE COVERINGS

Table coverings may range from a damask cloth with matching napkins to the place mat on the highly polished table to brightly colored cottons and linens—even pinks, browns and purples—to plastic tablecloths which can be easily wiped off. The kind of cloth that is used depends on the type of meal and the way it is served.

The important rule for a tablecloth is that it be clean. It is better to use a plastic covering which is spotless than a linen cloth which is soiled. Always check a tablecloth before putting it away to be used again, and follow the safe rule "When in doubt, don't."

The tablecloth is an important part of table setting and should fit the kind of meal that is served and the kind of dishes that are used. There are times when a white or pale colored cloth is used over table pads or a silence cloth. Such cloths usually have a generous overhang and have napkins which match them in color. If a lace or embroidered cloth is used, it is put over the bare wood and usually comes just to the edge of the table, though this is not a hard and fast rule. These do not have matching napkins.

Cotton and linen cloths, either white or colored and with matching or nonmatching napkins, are used for a great variety of entertaining. There really is no limit to the color combinations that may be used, although one would probably not use a patterned cloth with patterned dishes. Just as a white cloth with all white dishes might give a blah impression, a purple cloth used with dishes edged in pink roses and accompanied by green glasses might be too riotous a combination for some.

Place mats may be used at any time except for very formal service. They come in a variety of materials—cloth, plastic, straw or even paper—and are put on the bare wood with the edge of the mat almost at the edge of the table. All glasses and dishes must be kept on the place mat to avoid leaving marks on the wood.

CENTERPIECES

A centerpiece adds much to the eye appeal of a table. If one is used, it should be low enough that people can see across it to carry on a conversation. It should also be kept in proportion to the size of the table, and this may mean that sometimes there won't be a centerpiece because there isn't room for it. If candles are used, the flame should be either above or below eye level to keep from annoying anyone.

SETTING THE TABLE

The basics to remember in any table setting are a plate, a napkin, a water glass, a knife, a fork, and usually a spoon. Here again common sense dictates what dishes and silver are put on a table, for only those that are needed should be used.

Whether setting a table for a formal or an informal meal, the same basic arrangement is followed. (See further reference to the formal meal in the chapter on Entertaining.) The place settings around the table should be evenly spaced, allowing if possible twenty inches from one place to the next. This can't always be followed, of course, but one should try to have enough room so that people can eat comfortably and not feel crowded.

Each piece of silver is placed one inch from the edge of the table in the order it is to be used. Those pieces which are used first are farthest from the plate so that one begins on the outside and works in. The silver which is to be used in the right hand is on the right of the plate; that in the left hand, to the left (with the exception of a fish fork which may be put on either side). The cutting edge of the knife should be turned toward the plate. If there is to be no salad, then leave off the salad forks because it isn't necessary to put silver on the table which is not going to be used.

All the silver and dishes for each place should be close enough together to make a complete setting without looking crowded. The water glass is put above the point of the knife. The bread and butter plate is set above the fork, and the butter knife laid across the top edge with the spreading side toward the center of the plate. The salad plate goes to the left of the fork. If the table is crowded, one plate may serve both purposes or both may be omitted entirely and the salad and rolls put on the dinner plate. If the salad is the first course, the salad fork is put on the outside of the dinner fork; otherwise it may be either inside or outside. Usually if there is a small fork, then a large one and then a small one, it is assumed there will be salad, a main course, and a dessert which requires a fork.

The dessert fork or spoon is often laid on the table at the top of the dinner plate in a horizontal position, or is not brought in until the dessert is served. But it may as correctly be lined up with the rest of the silver. If a spoon is needed, it goes beside the knife; if a fork, it is put inside the dinner fork. An iced tea spoon may be put either beside the knife or on the right side of the saucer on which the glass of tea is set.

Most etiquette books say that the cups and saucers are not put on the table at the beginning of the meal because coffee or tea is not served with the dinner, or at least not until dessert. Actually many people prefer to have their beverage with their main course, and the hostess should allow guests a choice no matter what her personal preference is.

If the beverage is poured in the kitchen or by the hostess at the table, the cups and saucers would not be at each setting but placed for the convenience of the hostess. Or she may prefer to have them already at each place setting and pour for each person individually if there is room for her to go around the table. In any case, the spoons may be either already in place on the table or put on the side of the saucer.

THE PLACE PLATE

A place plate is used at each setting (always at a formal dinner or luncheon) to mark off each place and to avoid having an empty space before each guest. It is purely ornamental and is removed when the first course is brought in. In most of our informal serving we do not use a place plate or, if we do, it is as an underplate for a first course.

FOLDING A NAPKIN

It isn't necessary to fold a napkin in an elaborate or complicated way. A small napkin is left in a square while a large one may be folded in half or in a triangle shape and either put in the center of the setting (on the place plate if there is one) or laid beside the fork.

Here is an example of a properly set informal table which may be varied according to the requirements of the meal:

This basic pattern of table setting is the same for every meal regardless of the time or place.

Now of course when the husband is rushing to get off to work and the children to school, and the baby is banging on his high chair tray demanding his cereal, the wife is not going to set the table with underplates for the orange juice and bread and butter plates for the toast. But neither is it necessary to set the gallon milk jug on the table and line up a row of giant-sized cereal boxes just because it is more convenient to serve that way. The table can be neatly set with the coffee cream and cereal milk in pitchers and the jelly in a serving dish. The same principle applies to other meals.

There must be orderliness in setting the table and in serving and eating the food. This is true not just for special entertaining, but also for the informal and family entertaining which we do every day. Even serving picnic style with paper plates and plastic forks should be neat and orderly because being casual and informal does not mean being careless and sloppy. A table should look as though someone cared about setting it right, rather than just throwing it together hit or miss.

SEATING GUESTS

There are several ways of seating guests at a table. The usual way is to seat the host at the head of the table, the hostess at the foot (usually the end of the table nearest the kitchen), and the guests down each side as in the following illustration:

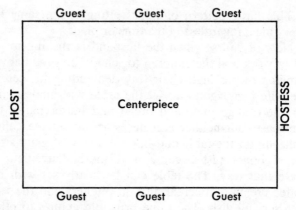

Or the host and hostess may sit in the middle on each side of the table with the guests on either side of them as in this example:

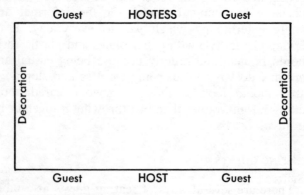

This leaves both ends of the table empty and allows for two balancing decorative arrangements. An advantage to this seating plan is that it brings host and hostess closer to the guests for more ease in conversation.

GUEST OF HONOR

It has been traditional for the woman guest of honor to sit at the right of the host and the man guest of honor at the right of the hostess. But often there isn't any special guest at most informal dinners so that the oldest ones present or those who are guests for the first time or just anybody may be seated in these positions. Unless there is special protocol that must be followed as for a formal meal, one may seat guests in any order. It isn't necessary to always separate husbands and wives, nor is it even necessary to alternate men and women around the table except that this often helps to stimulate conversation.

SERVING FOOD

The food may be served in any way one likes and according to what is most convenient for the hostess and the guests. One way that is frequently used is the family style in which the serving dishes are passed around the table for each one to help himself. Or the host may carve the meat and serve it on the plates which are then either passed to the hostess who serves the rest of the food, or given to the guests who help themselves to the potatoes and vegetables. If this style is followed, it is better to have the plates stacked in front of the host rather than at each place, to avoid passing and repassing them. Sometimes the hostess serves the meat, which has been previously carved in the kitchen. Often the hostess prefers to fill the plates in the kitchen and bring them to the table for each person. One may also follow the buffet style of serving which is described in the chapter on Entertaining.

There is sometimes uncertainty about how food should be served and the dishes removed from the table. This really isn't complicated, for one may either serve and remove everything from the left except the beverage, or serve from the left and remove from the right. The point is to do this in as convenient a way as possible for everyone concerned. Therefore it would be better not to reach across a person from the left to remove the water glass nor across from the right to take away his salad plate.

CLEARING THE TABLE

When the table is cleared for the dessert, the serving dishes, if any, are removed first and then the dinner plates and other used dishes. Everything should be cleared except the water glasses and cups and saucers (if a hot beverage has been served with the main course).

It is sometimes necessary to adjust rules and forms to one's own particular style of living. But even though the parents and four children have to eat all their meals around a small table in the kitchen, gracious dining does not have to be completely sacrificed. It should be a part of everyday life insofar as possible and not kept just for company. The family ought to receive guest attention every day in the care that is taken to set the table as nicely as possible and in the loving attention that is given to the preparation of the food.

Such a gracious atmosphere doesn't depend on expensive settings of china, crystal and silver nor on elaborate and expensive food. It is based on knowing how to make the best use of what one has even if this best is a plastic tablecloth, earthenware mugs and stainless steel utensils. If these are used with an eye to balance and color harmony and orderliness, the table will be well set. One should develop one's own distinctive style in this and not be just a carbon of someone else.

MONOGRAMMING SILVER

As we think of linens and silver, it's well to remember that it isn't necessary to monogram anything, not even silver, unless one wishes to. In fact, when buying a gift for a bride, it is better to leave it unmarked unless you are sure how she wishes to have it monogrammed and know which style she prefers. Many women like to use their maiden initials as the monogram, and of course do so if they begin to buy silver before they are engaged. It's also correct to use either one or all of one's married initials. Others like the idea of combining the first initial of each name with the man's last initial.

So when Mary Louise Smith and Richard Paul Jones are married, their silver may be marked with an S, with MLS, MSJ (Mary Smith Jones), J, or MRJ (also MJR). If only one letter is used, it is an initial and not a monogram. How it is arranged is a matter of personal preference, though the monogram, whether it is on the upper or underside (of silverware), should blend with the lines of the handle. If the handle is fairly wide, the monogram could be MJR or MJR. If it is slender, the monogram might better be arranged in a triangle as $M_J R$ or $_M{}^J{}_R$. Generally, script monograms look best on traditional silver patterns, and block letters on modern patterns. However it is done, it remains a matter of individual taste. Usually it is only sterling that is monogrammed, although one could certainly do so to plate and stainless if one cared to.

In any discussion of the proper way to do things, even in this matter of setting the table and serving food, we need to reemphasize the importance of the spirit which should motivate all our actions. Nothing that we do should be ostentatious and done just to impress others. It is not the possession of money but the love of it that God warns is the root of all evil. This can apply to all the things that we have. We should not make either the possession of things or the lack of them something to be proud of.

6

ENTERTAINING

One of the requirements in Scripture for a leader in the church is that he be "given to hospitality" (I Timothy 3:2). This includes gracious care for the stranger as well as for the close friend. The Lord Jesus even suggested that one should not entertain only those who could easily repay an invitation, but even more those who could not. He said in doing this "thou shalt be blessed" (Luke 14:13-14).

REASONS FOR ENTERTAINING

Entertaining is a broad term that includes the formal dinner, the afternoon tea, the informal dinner, the casual spur-of-the moment picnic or the morning coffee klatch. The purpose should be to have a good time with friends. This purpose is defeated if the hostess uses entertaining to repay a list of social obligations, and this is partly what the Lord was referring to in Luke 14.

The purpose of entertaining is also defeated if we worry too much about the externals of a beautiful house and nice furnishings. We sometimes deprive ourselves of friendships when we hesitate to entertain because of a limited budget or because our house is not as well furnished as our neighbor's. If the house is clean, and warmth and friendliness are there, the furnishings are not important.

RETURNING INVITATIONS

Perhaps we would entertain more often if we remembered that it isn't necessary to return an invitation exactly as we received one. If you were invited to someone's home for dinner, it's perfectly all right to return an invitation to an after-church supper or for dessert and coffee in the evening. Doing what one is able is the important thing. Of course, while a dinner invitation does not require a dinner in return, you might not return it by a picnic supper either, because some people are simply not picnic people. This is where sensitivity to others, an important part of etiquette, applies even in the realm of entertaining.

SIMPLICITY

Our day is one of simplicity, of informality, of more casual behavior in almost every area of life. Smaller homes, more automatic equipment and the trend to outdoor eating contribute toward a more relaxed view of entertaining. This casual view is reflected not only in the kind of entertaining we do but also in the china, glassware and silver we use. (See chapter on Table Setting.) Obviously how we handle a buffet picnic supper is not the way we would plan a four-course sit-down dinner, nor do we plan a bridesmaids' luncheon in the same way as a child's birthday party.

DIFFERENT WAYS TO ENTERTAIN

Entertaining is a realm where the hostess' imagination can have free rein and still be within the framework of good taste and correct etiquette. Good taste and correct etiquette mean doing the right thing in the right way at the right time. Since none of us is born knowing what is the right way and time and place, we must learn through observation and practice.

There are a time and a place for many different kinds of entertaining both of guests and family. Sometimes we eat in full regalia at the dining room table using the best china and silver. Sometimes we eat at the kitchen table or in the breakfast room, sometimes while perched on high stools at the snack bar, occasionally from trays in the living room by the fireplace, and sometimes at a picnic table in the backyard. The place and the type of utensils used are not the important ingredients; what matters is that the atmosphere be pleasant and relaxed and warm.

Too often we save for guests the little extra touches which turn an ordinary meal into a party. Dinner is often the only time of the day when the family is complete, and that time should be used to strengthen family oneness. This should automatically rule out the too-frequent meals on trays before a blaring television set.

Yet even though we always plan carefully for the family, we naturally do some extra things when we have guests. These depend on the way we choose to entertain.

FORMAL ENTERTAINING

One way is the formal dinner or luncheon. Formal entertaining in the strict sense of the word refers to the way food is served, rather than to the china or silverware that is used. The food is always served to the guests. If they help themselves from dishes that are passed from hand to hand around the table, if the host carves the meat and serves the plates, or if the hostess has any part in bringing the food to the table or clearing it away, it is not a formal meal.

Most of us may feel that we will never have a formal meal since we do not have a maid to serve. But it is well to know the distinguishing features of a formal dinner since we may be guests at one sometime and we should know what to expect. Then too it is possible to hire temporary help if we should ever be required to entertain formally.

When an invitation to a formal meal is sent through the mail (sometimes it is telephoned), it is always in the third person and should be answered that way. (See chapter on Correspondence.) A formal dinner requires full evening dress. Place cards are used on the table, each lady is escorted to the dining room by her partner for the evening, and there are usually six or seven courses.

The tablecloth must be a full size with a generous overhang, and large dinner napkins must match the cloth. A white or very pale colored damask cloth is put either over pads which fit the table or over a silence cloth (this may be a sheet cut to fit the top of the table). There is always a centerpiece on a formally set table, whether flowers and candles or other decorative objects. The dishes are always fine china and the silver must be sterling. All the plates and dishes used for each course must match, although different sets may be used for some of the courses rather than the same pattern used throughout the meal. The formal dinner or luncheon is very ceremonious, very traditional, very elegant.

INFORMAL DINNER

However, it is the informal dinner that most of us give and attend. Guests are usually invited verbally or by an informal note. The dishes and silver need not be fine china and sterling, though the table may be set just as beautifully and elegantly. Evening clothes are seldom worn. Usually only three or four courses are served, and the host and hostess have some part in serving the meal. The same basic principles are followed in setting the table whether it is a formal or informal meal. (See chapter on Table Setting.)

An informal dinner may have three courses, consisting of an appetizer of soup, fruit or juice; a main course (meat and salad); dessert; or four courses of appetizer, salad, main course and dessert; or five courses of fruit or fish (such as shrimp cocktail), soup, main course, salad and dessert. The informal dinner may be just a casual buffet supper, and between it and the formal dinner are many variations with much overlapping of the two extremes.

This doesn't mean that any informal element can be brought into the formal meal, because then it would not be formal. But some of the formal elements of orderliness and style can be used to enhance even the casual serving of a meal.

Even though we all entertain informally often, it is well to review some of the principles of how best to do it. In brief, these are to plan the kind of entertaining you can do best, don't worry about what you don't have, and invite people you enjoy being with.

EASIER ENTERTAINING

Sometimes we dread entertaining because of the work involved in planning the menu, cleaning the house, preparing the food and straightening up afterward. After all, careful planning and extra work are necessary even though only a few friends are invited. If the hostess prepares and serves the meal alone, the menu should be one she is sure of and one that does not require a great deal of last-minute attention. If we keep in mind that the purpose of entertaining is to have friendly contacts with others, and if we entertain in keeping with what we can do easily and well, it will not be such a formidable chore.

Of course the working woman who tries to put on a five-course dinner for sixteen all by herself is going to run into some frustrating moments. And of course the inexperienced bride who tries to entertain the boss and his wife by serving a French meal is going to dissolve in tears somewhere along the line. But this is putting on false pretensions and almost deserves to fail. It would be much better to serve the boss Italian spaghetti, crusty French bread, a tossed salad, lemon ice and brownies until she has had more practice with the fancy recipes.

It is possible to have help to make entertaining easier. One of the best sources is one's own children if they are old enough (and even quite a small child can run the vacuum cleaner). Instead of shooing them out of the way, let them set the table, prepare salads, butter the rolls, and dice the chicken, for this is good experience for them.

HIRING HELP

Other sources of help are neighbor girls and college girls who can be hired to baby-sit, or to come in to wash the dishes. There are also professional part-time maids and waitresses who advertise their services in local papers. The rates paid for such help depend on the kind of work you expect them to do, how long you want them and where you live. If you have a fancy house in an expensive suburb, you'll have to pay more than if you live in a small house nearer the city.

USING A CATERER

It is also possible to have a party or dinner catered, which means anyone can serve a formal meal because a caterer will take over completely and furnish everything, including people to serve the meal. However, when engaging a caterer, it is wise to discuss with him fully the kind of meal you want, the menu, how it will be served, and his price. Ask to see his equipment, because not all catering services will meet your standard of excellence.

SECRETS OF SUCCESSFUL ENTERTAINING

It is important that the hostess be relaxed whether she is entertaining with or without help. She should keep the house reasonably clean always so that a frenzy of extra work is not needed, check the silver often enough to know that every piece won't have to be cleaned the day before it is used, be sure all table-cloths are put away ready for use, plan a menu she is confident won't go wrong, and prepare in advance as much as possible. These are the main secrets of successful entertaining. Then, even if things don't turn out just right because the soufflé which never fails, did, and the always tender pastry is tough, don't apologize—at least not too much.

There are ways of making the serving of a sit-down meal go smoothly. A first course served in the living room, whether it is just tomato juice and a cracker or something more fancy, helps to speed the service of the next course at the table. The main part of the meal may be served in any way which is most convenient. (See chapter on Table Setting.) Every hostess has to work this out for herself, adapting serving rules to her own needs. If space is really limited at the table, most of the main course could be served on one platter, such as a mound of rice or noodles in the center flanked by chops or steak or even slices of meat loaf alternating with a green vegetable. A salad and rolls on the dinner plate use the available space effectively.

STATING A CHOICE

Most of us are pretty careful of our manners when we are guests in someone's home, but there is one place where both hostess and guests sometimes err. The hostess should not urge her guests repeatedly to take more of something once they have refused a second helping. Not taking more is no reflection on the cooking; it is just good sense to stop when you have had enough. And guests, when given a choice of, say coffee or tea, should make a choice. The answer "Whichever is easier" or "Whichever you have" is no answer at all. The hostess would not give a choice if she were not prepared to follow through, and it is annoying to have this kind of response. It sounds polite and considerate, but it really isn't.

If the hostess who serves alone has planned well, she will not need to leave the table until time to clear the main course and bring in the dessert. Of course, if the meal is served family style, the dishes will have to be replenished and the water glasses refilled, and this is the duty of the hostess. But she should try to leave the table as little as possible.

CLEARING THE TABLE

All serving dishes, used plates, salt and pepper, and condiment dishes are removed before the dessert is brought in. This should be done as quickly and efficiently as possible whether by taking several plates at a time to the kitchen (preferably not scraped and stacked at the table) or by putting used dishes on a serving cart and wheeling it to the kitchen.

It isn't usually necessary to crumb the table since most people eat reasonably neatly. If a guest sees that he has a lot of bread crumbs at his place, he can pick them up and put them on his plate before it is removed without making a fuss about it. The dessert plate will be brought in right away anyway and will probably cover any little jelly or gravy stain that all of us make at some time or other.

The coffee is usually served with the dessert at the table. But even so, it is pleasant to move away from the table and have a leisurely second cup in the living room. If this is done, the coffee and tea and the cream and sugar should be ready on a large tray which is put on a table near where the hostess will sit to pour it.

WASHING DISHES

Ordinarily a hostess should be very firm about not accepting help with the dishes. If guests have been invited for an evening of relaxation, dishes should not be part of the plans no matter how much the hostess may hate to face them later that evening or in the morning. There are times when help may be accepted, but a guest should not insist if his first polite offer is refused. Naturally those who have automatic dish-washers will find this part of entertaining simplified. There is no reason why the host cannot keep the conversation going while the dinner dishes are quickly rinsed and loaded into the washer before the dessert is served. You will have to be your own judge as to the feasibility of this, and you may not want to try it unless you are really speedy and the guests are good friends. Most hostesses will at least take time to whisk leftover food into the refrigerator.

BUFFET SERVICE

Because many homes do not have dining rooms large enough to entertain guests comfortably at a seated meal, other types of entertaining have become popular. One of these is buffet service, which makes it possible for a hostess to serve more guests at one time than would be possible at a sit-down meal. However, buffet serving requires careful planning.

Buffet entertaining is not a thrown together, eat-any-way-you-want meal even though it might be served from the kitchen table. If this too-casual spirit is the way in which it is done, it will not be successful buffet service. There are really very few rules about how to serve buffet style other than that the food be attractively arranged, the table not be overcrowded, the guests be able to help themselves easily, and places be provided for each guest to sit.

It isn't wise to invite more people to a buffet meal than can be adequately seated even though they need not all be around one table. There are several ways of seating people when serving buffet style. One way is to put them at small tables in the living room or family room. The tables should be already set with a small centerpiece, perhaps only a slender bud vase with a flower, and with silver, napkins and coffee cups already at each place. It's usually best not to include water glasses because of space limitations. The guests first serve themselves food from the buffet table, then seat themselves at the small tables where the beverage is served to them.

Or guests may serve themselves at the buffet table and then be seated all together at a large table which is set as the small tables just described. In this case there would be room for water glasses, and the centerpiece could be larger.

If there isn't room to set up small tables, guests help themselves from the buffet table, including napkins, silver and beverage, and then carry their filled plates to another room to eat. Everyone must have a place to sit, and someplace, preferably not the floor, on which to set glasses and cups.

Whatever method of seating is used, the food must be the kind that can be easily handled on a plate, eaten without too much difficulty, and must not require too many utensils. There are no courses as such because all the food, except the dessert, is laid out at one time, but there should be an abundance and a good variety. Casseroles and stews which are easily kept hot, a baked ham, already buttered rolls or bread, a variety of salads, cold meats, cheeses and relishes are all good buffet foods. It is important, however, that cold foods be kept cold and hot foods hot. Guests should be free to return and help themselves as often as they wish, and nothing is more unappetizing than returning to a melted salad or cold beef stroganoff.

Dessert may either be served directly to each guest by the hostess, or the table may be cleared and the dessert laid out for the guests to help themselves.

Careful attention should be given to the arrangement and setting of the buffet table. It may be formal or informal; set in the kitchen, dining room or enclosed porch; have crystal and sterling or pottery dishes and stainless steel utensils. Even the centerpiece does not have to be flowers and candles if a bowl of fresh fruit looks just as well and may be a part of the dessert. What matters is that the result be an attractive and eye-pleasing picture.

Keep in mind the ease with which the guests can serve themselves. Put all the hot foods together with whatever should be served with them, then all the salads and dressings, the rolls, the relishes and preserves, and so on. Have the plates stacked so that they may be taken first, the napkins arranged to be easily picked up. If the silver is to be taken from the table, it should be laid out last, or it could be wrapped in the napkin to be picked up all at once.

It should be possible to move around the buffet table easily without bumping into others. In smaller houses this will require careful planning and perhaps shifting around of furniture. Usually to do this the table should be in the center of the room so that traffic can flow around it easily.

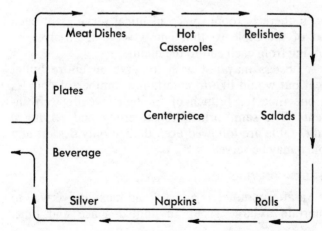

Meat Dishes	Hot Casseroles	Relishes
Plates		
	Centerpiece	Salads
Beverage		
Silver	Napkins	Rolls

If this arrangement isn't possible, push the table against the wall and lay the food along the length of it, perhaps having the dishes several widths deep as long as they can be conveniently reached.

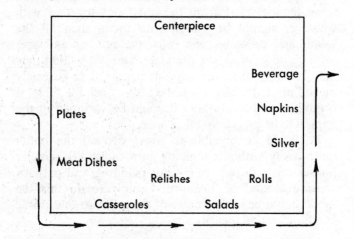

Or, if there is room, place identical servings at each end of the table so that guests serve themselves by moving from each end to the middle.

A hostess may not wish to serve an entire buffet meal but would like to entertain a number of couples at one time for brunch or for light evening refreshments. The same principles of setting and serving a buffet table are followed even though only dessert and coffee may be served.

AFTERNOON TEAS

An afternoon tea is an easy and inexpensive way to entertain a large group in limited space and time.

These are usually friendly and informal, though often, when given by an organization or a club, they are quite formal. A tea may be given to welcome a new daughter-in-law or a new neighbor, as a housewarming, or for no particular reason at all. If space in the house is really limited, coffee and tea may be served individually on trays or small plates; but usually a tea table is set very attractively with the best china and silver. It should be covered with a pretty cloth (a lace one over a bare table is the nicest), with flowers and candles as the centerpiece. Since no one sits at the table except those who are pouring at either end, the centerpiece may be as high and elaborate as will look well with the surroundings. Even though it is still daylight, be sure the candles are lighted for they add so much to the festive atmosphere.

A large tray with a coffee and tea service is set at either end of the table. If the group is small, one person may serve both from the same tray. The cups and saucers should be within easy reach of those who are pouring and someone should be responsible for keeping a fresh supply always ready. The best position for them is on the left of the tray with the handles toward the one pouring. Since one would use the daintiest cups one owns, it is better not to pile them together. At either end of the table should be a stack of small plates with napkins and spoons. Sometimes plates are not provided and guests are expected to balance a cookie on the edge of a saucer. It's much better to use large enough plates to hold a cup as well as a cookie and a sandwich and nuts. One could also use the little snack trays of glass or china which are very attractive and handy.

Then, in any arrangement the hostess wishes as long as it does not look cluttered, will be the plates of tiny cakes, petits fours, finger sandwiches and dishes of mints and nuts. Such a tea table will look like this:

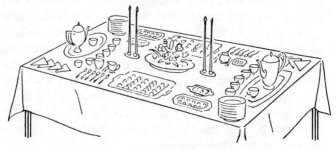

Those who are asked to pour at a large tea generally do so for about thirty minutes and then someone else takes over. For a small tea the same one may pour the entire time people are being served. It is easy to pour coffee or tea while seated, but if punch is served, it may be easier to do so standing up.

Invitations to a tea may be phoned, or sent on informals or on fill-in invitation cards. RSVP is not included, although an answer is courteous. If a very large group is to be entertained at a tea, it may be divided in half, with one group coming from one to three o'clock and the other from three to five o'clock. This should be specified on the invitation, of course.

Women usually wear dressy street clothes with hats (optional) and gloves, and carry bags. One may stay as briefly as one wishes, but must always thank the hostess before leaving. Men are seldom free to attend an afternoon tea, but if they are included, the food is somewhat more substantial than just cookies and tiny cakes.

COFFEES

The same basic formula is followed for a coffee, which may be given either morning or afternoon depending on the custom of the community one lives in. If a coffee is held before noon, coffee cakes, sweet rolls or fruit breads are served rather than cakes and cookies. A coffee may be quite as elaborate as the afternoon tea, or it may be only coffee and a sweet roll at the kitchen table with a couple of neighbors. The same spirit of friendliness should be the motivation of each.

EVENING COFFEE AND DESSERT

Another easy way to entertain is by inviting friends in for coffee and dessert in the evening. When this is the invitation, it should be just that and no more although this is a time to plan a really spectacular dessert, since it is the only food to be prepared. Even though this is the dessert everyone skipped at dinner, it does not have to be served early in the evening unless you want to do so. What you do for entertainment during the evening depends on you and your guests. Conversation still remains one of the most stimulating ways to spend an evening if it's carried on in the right way. (See chapter on Conversation.) Some people like to play word games or put puzzles together. Some would prefer to sit and watch television, but this is not entertaining in the real meaning of the word. Unless there is a particular program in which everyone is interested, it's better not to turn on the TV, because everyone could just as well have stayed home and looked at his own set.

OPEN HOUSE

An open house is an informal gathering of friends, relatives and neighbors over a stated four- or five-hour period. Many people entertain in this way once a year, perhaps at Christmas or New Year, as an established family custom. Since an answer is never expected to an invitation to an open house, the refreshments must be ample enough for all who might come. If the open house is held between lunch and dinner, the food is usually small fancy sandwiches, cakes, cookies, coffee, tea and/or punch. If it is held over the dinner hour or in the early evening, more substantial food must be provided. Then it really becomes a buffet supper and the principles that govern buffet serving apply to it.

SHOWERS

Showers are given for a variety of reasons though the usual ones are to honor a bride-to-be or to welcome a new baby. Sometimes a new minister and his family are welcomed by a pantry shower, which is just what the name implies. Showers may be given at any time during the day or evening. The chief feature is that those attending bring gifts to the guest of honor.

A bridal shower is never given by a member of the bride's immediate family, that is, her sisters or mother or grandmother, since everyone who comes is expected to bring a gift. If you are invited and cannot go, you are not obligated to send a gift. However, it is well to follow the custom of your community in this. And, of course, you may want to give a gift anyway, if you are a close friend.

A shower gift is supposed to be a small, fairly inexpensive item. This is not always so, because sometimes friends give a more expensive gift and consider it as a wedding gift also. Should friends join in giving one large item? This is often welcome at a baby shower when a high chair or bathinette is needed. But a shower implies a variety of smaller gifts; the larger one could be given as a wedding present.

Bridal showers become a problem if too many are given for the same girl so that they become a financial drain on her friends. This can be controlled by the mother of the bride-to-be or by the girl herself suggesting that she has already had several and no more are needed. If someone wants to honor her anyway and give a shower, the invitations could read "recipe shower" or "Bring household hints" instead of the usual "kitchen" or "linen" or "personal" notation.

The person(s) giving the shower should include on the invitation the name of the store(s) where the bride is registered and her color preferences if she has decided on them. For example: "Bathroom—green and gold; kitchen—lime and tangerine."

Only light refreshments are needed at a shower since men are generally not present. The setting should be gay, festive and colorful in keeping with the spirit of the party. (See the chapter on Weddings for plans for a wedding reception.)

BARBECUES

Barbecues are an easy, informal way of accommodating a large number of guests during the warm weather if one's house is too small to serve more than a few people. Cooking the meat to the specifications of the individual guest is part of the fun, and it is usually the most important part of the meal. The rest of the food is generally prepared inside ahead of time and is typical picnic food which can be eaten with a minimum of table service. Hamburgers, barbecued chicken, thick steaks, corn on the cob, potato salad and fresh fruit are foods we associate with a barbecue or outdoor grill.

The informality of the outdoor atmosphere can be carried over into the table setting and decorations. A plastic tablecloth or a checked gingham cloth or even a paper covering is good. An ample supply of paper napkins is needed since much of the food is the finger-eating kind. This is a time when plastic-coated plates are appropriate and even plastic forks and knives, though the latter are not recommended if the meat must be cut. Everyone should have a place to sit. One of the most important ingredients for the success of an outdoor barbecue is a supply of insect repellent.

COVERED DISH SUPPER

Most people are familiar with a potluck or covered dish meal, which is a method of entertaining that is practical for a church group or club, or even for neighbors getting together in one home or backyard for a meal. It is just what the name implies since each one brings a dish of food to contribute to the common table. To avoid having six spaghetti dishes and one potato salad, it's usually wise to ask several to bring a salad, some a casserole, and others a dessert. This kind of meal may be very informal, with picnic style table setting and serving procedures, particularly if it is eaten outdoors. If the table is set indoors, general buffet serving rules apply to the potluck meal.

PROGRESSIVE DINNER

A progressive dinner is a way to entertain that is fun for those taking part but wearing on the ingenuity of those doing the planning, for it means that a group of people go to a different home for each separate course. If four couples are planning a progressive dinner, everyone will meet at the first house for the appetizer, at the second for the salad course, at the third for the main course, and at the fourth house for the dessert. If it is a large group, the planning is more complicated. One way of working out the arrangements for this kind of meal for a club or church organization or Sunday school class is to have everyone meet in one home for the appetizer. This could be just tomato juice and a cracker and no one would have to be seated. Then divide the group into three or four smaller groups for a salad course, and then into groups of only four or six for a sit-down main course. After this everyone would meet together in one place, perhaps the church fellowship room or a rented hall, for the dessert and a program or social time of some sort. Those who did not entertain during any of the first courses could bring the pies or cakes or whatever for the dessert. If everyone entertained in some way, then each couple would contribute to the dessert.

CHILDREN'S PARTIES

Children's parties should have one rule above all others—simplicity. Save the fancy, elaborate decorations and food for adults who will appreciate them. Parties for very young children should be brief and uncomplicated. Two- and three-year-olds have not learned to play together well, so there is little use in having organized games. Only the simplest of refreshments, milk and a cookie, or a small dish of ice cream, or jello and a cookie, are all that are needed.

Parties for older children require more planning. Since children like to receive mail, it's a good idea to send out invitations. This serves the double purpose of giving parents necessary information as to time and place. Be definite about the hours, making clear that the party is from "3:00-5:00 P.M." or "We'll bring Billy home at 7:30." Plan quiet games as well as active ones, and be prepared for noise. If prizes are given, it's a good idea to have something that everyone can take home. The menu for children's parties is neither hard to plan nor expensive because hot dogs, hamburgers or sloppy joes; potato chips or french fries; pickles, carrot and celery strips; and ice cream and cake are standard fare.

A party is not a place continually to remind a child to say thank you for a present, or to remind him not to grab the biggest piece of cake. But it is a place where, hopefully, a child will remember to practice the manners he has already learned. (See chapter on Children and Teenagers.)

HAVING OVERNIGHT OR WEEKEND GUESTS

There are special obligations which fall on the host and hostess when they invite someone to stay overnight or for the weekend. In fact, one should think twice before extending an impromptu overnight invitation. Many a visiting preacher has shared a room with a small child, or spent an uncomfortable night on the living room couch with the family dog sniffing at him suspiciously, because of the generosity of someone who really was not equipped to entertain an overnight guest. In a case like this, the minister should be given the courtesy of an overnight in a hotel or motel with the cordiality of the congregation showing itself in other ways.

Of course, not many people have a room always standing ready for use. Often a den or a sewing room must double as an extra bedroom. Sometimes the children may have to move into sleeping bags on the living room floor or on the porch so that their room(s) can be temporary guest room quarters. Whatever the arrangements, be sure the room for the guest has drawer space, closet space, enough hangers, a clock and good lighting.

Whenever guests are invited, particularly for the weekend, let them know what hours meals are served. Tell them in advance what the plans are so they will know what clothes to bring. Be definite as to when they should come and, equally important, when they are expected to leave. This can all be contained within the invitation whether given verbally or written. For example:

Dear Jane,

We are hoping you will be able to come for the weekend visit you've been promising us. Come as early as you can Friday afternoon, though dinner will not be until seven since Bob is usually late getting home. Plan to stay until late Sunday evening, because we're inviting the Smiths in for coffee after church.

Bob is eager to try out his new golf clubs Saturday morning, so be sure Ted brings his. We have tickets for a concert at the college that evening.

Love,

Mary

Even though you will make plans for the weekend when you have guests, don't fill up every minute of the time, both for your sake and theirs.

OBLIGATIONS OF OVERNIGHT GUEST

But the overnight or weekend guest has obligations also. He should arrive and leave when expected, not borrow personal items such as toothpaste and shampoo, and not monopolize the bathroom or the telephone. He must be prompt for meals even if they are at hours when he does not ordinarily eat. A woman guest should plan to dress for breakfast even if at home she appears in bathrobe and curlers and doesn't mind if *her* guests do.

Whether you are visiting people who are practically strangers or are spending a week with your own parents, make your own bed and keep your room straightened up (and the bathroom). Whatever other help you give depends on the situation, but if your first polite offers are refused, don't insist. The hostess may already have done all the dusting she thinks is necessary; or she likes the way she washes the lettuce better than the way you do it, and may prefer that you just sit and visit with her. If she has prepared sufficiently for you, she will have to do only the bare minimum of work herself in getting the meals ready. If you feel that you are being a burden to her, then she has failed in her responsibility to you.

TAKING A GIFT

Most overnight or weekend guests like to bring the hostess a gift. Flowers or a box of candy are always welcome, but they are so usual. Try bringing a plant which may be set out in the garden if the hostess wishes, or a pretty apron, or a set of pot holders. Other suggestions are a pair of hand-embroidered guest towels, a box of pretty cakes of soap, a jar of gourmet food, a cookbook of unusual recipes, or a box of extra-nice stationery. If there are children in the family, a small gift to them is appreciated by the hostess almost more than one to herself. You might prefer to wait until after your visit and send a gift of something you have observed she might like.

A gift is not strictly necessary, but a thank you note very definitely is, and must be written within a few days after you have returned home. (See chapter on Correspondence.)

All of us enjoy having fellowship with those "of like precious faith," and so we enjoy entertaining our friends. But entertaining can also be an outreach. The neighbor or business acquaintance who would never attend church to hear the gospel would probably come to your home for a barbecue or for dessert and coffee some evening. Because of this his life could be changed.

Entertaining is given a new dimension if, because we invited someone to dinner, he finds Christ as his Saviour. Then he with us will eventually be a part of the great marriage supper of the Lamb spoken of in Revelation 19.

7

DATING AND ENGAGEMENTS

There are very definite instructions in the Word of God concerning the behavior of Christians. The admonitions apply to each of us in every situation of life: "Whatsoever ye do, do all to the glory of God. Give none offence" (I Corinthians 10:31-32). "Giving no offence in any thing, that the ministry be not blamed" (II Corinthians 6:3). Young people who are dating are particularly vulnerable and especially need this reminder from God.

DATING PROPRIETIES

This is a fascinating and controversial subject. In the past, society condemned those who broke the rules surrounding behavior between men and women. But our day and culture have brought a freedom between the sexes which has changed some of the old customs of dating. The automobile provides a mobility which takes young people from the shelter of home and chaperon. This puts a greater responsibility on the dating couple to behave properly so as to "give none offence."

Of course, a chaperon ought only to be needed for appearance' sake, because young people, and especially those who are believers, should have an innate sense of propriety which in itself would be a sufficient chaperon. Yet the temptations of love can blind even a Christian couple to the potential dangers in a too-close relationship before marriage. Aside from the possible temptations, there is still the appearance to others which must be considered. There are always those who will misinterpret a situation no matter how innocent it actually may be. (See chapter on Children and Teenagers.)

The Christian couple should have another motive in maintaining pure standards and this is found in the reference in II Corinthians 6:3. Each one has the personal responsibility of avoiding any behavior which will bring the ministry, and more specifically the Lord Jesus Christ, into disrepute.

Dating now often begins at an earlier age than ever before, allowed by parents who find it easier to go along with the "but everyone else does" plea than to think through reasonable rules for their own children. Regardless of the age, there are certain proprieties to be observed by those who are dating, which cover a wide range of situations. These proprieties have stood through the years and are still right even in our day of relaxed standards. The fact that they are not always observed does not mean they should therefore be thrown away.

What makes a date depends on many things, including the couple's own attitude toward it. It doesn't have to be an expensive, dressed up, night-out-on-the-town kind of thing. A coke at the drugstore on the way home from school can be as satisfying as a banquet at a hotel with a formal and a tuxedo. Dating is one good way for teenagers to learn to put the proper value on what is really important in life. A good time doesn't always mean filet mignon in an expensive restaurant or a ride in a convertible.

ASKING FOR A DATE IN ADVANCE

One of the proprieties in dating that girls appreciate is to have the boy phone far enough in advance for a date so that she can plan for it. Most girls like to be asked at least a week ahead for a casual date and more than that for something formal. The invitation should be definite. Don't ask, "What are you doing Saturday night?" because a girl hates to say, "Nothing," which might then commit her to something she doesn't want to do. Instead say, "I've got two tickets for the game Saturday. Can you go with me?" Making the invitation specific helps a girl to know what to wear. No girl wants to turn up in dressy clothes when everyone else is wearing a skirt and sweater.

DRESSING FOR A DATE

Naturally one dresses for a date according to where one goes and what one does. This means sport clothes for a picnic, bowling, a bike hike or a beach party; school clothes for the casual afternoon and evening dates during the week; dressy clothes for dinner in a restaurant, going to church or to the youth rally; and really dressing up for the formal youth banquet or whatever.

CORSAGES

When a corsage is in order, the man finds out in

advance what color dress the girl will be wearing so that his choice of flowers will not clash with it. If he hasn't done so and the color combination is really awful, she must accept the corsage graciously anyway, hard as this is, and wear it, if not on her dress, then attached to a bracelet or pinned on a small evening bag. When flowers are worn on the dress, put them on the way they grow—straight up. A corsage may be brought by the man when he calls for his date, but it's better to have it sent in advance to give the girl time to put it on—and to get over the shock if it isn't what she expected.

DATES WHILE BABY-SITTING

The matter of having a date while baby-sitting can be a tricky situation. Some employers don't mind and give their permission for a boyfriend to come over and keep the baby-sitter company. Others object strenuously, particularly if it is done without their knowledge. This is another case where a dating couple must be careful not to give offense. After all, even having another girl come in to help baby-sit does not necessarily mean extra protection for the children. Two girls can get so involved in conversation that they forget their responsibilities.

What should a girl do when a boy she would really like to go out with calls her, but she already has a date for that evening, or is committed to a family project, or has a baby-sitting job she can't break? She has to turn him down, of course, but with enough regret in her voice that he'll know she isn't just making up an excuse. Girls usually think they have the hard time in the dating game because they have to wait around for the boy to call them, and they envy him his privilege of doing so or not as he wishes. But a boy too has a hard time getting up nerve enough to call, not knowing if he will be turned down.

Another reason why many boys hesitate to date is that girls often take a casual date too seriously and expect one to be followed by others. If more dating by teenagers were on a friendship basis, the girls might find they were asked out more often.

GIRLS PHONING BOYS

Ordinarily a girl does not call a boy on the telephone, but this can't be made an absolute rule. There are legitimate reasons for calling—to take care of business for a committee they may both be on, to check on a homework assignment, to make plans for a youth program at church. But calling in the hope of making a date remains the privilege of the boy, who doesn't want the girl to do it. A couple who are going steady or are engaged may have their own understanding about this, of course.

GOING STEADY

So much emphasis has been put on dating that the girl or boy who doesn't date seriously during high school feels out of it socially. This has given rise to the custom of going steady, which means that a couple date each other to the exclusion of everyone else whether this lasts one week or a month, or becomes permanent in marriage. This system has the advantage that a couple always has a date for anything that comes along, and it eliminates the agony on the girl's part of wondering if she will have a date, and on the boy's, of wondering whom to ask for a date. But it has the disadvantage of narrowing the circle of friendships too drastically and allowing two people to become too familiar with each other before they are ready for marriage. There are often emotional scars when a steady couple breaks up.

REFUSING A DATE

When a girl is asked for a date by someone she really doesn't want to go out with, it isn't necessary for her to think up elaborate excuses. A polite but firm "I'm sorry, I can't, but thanks for calling" is enough. Even if the boy calls several times, he will soon take the hint and stop. And of course it is never right to accept a date tentatively or to keep a boy dangling while hoping that something better will turn up. It isn't a smart idea to cancel an already made date with a phony excuse in order to go out with someone else. Even if the first boy never finds out, it still isn't good manners. Anything like this is wrong for a Christian because it is a lie no matter what else it might be called in excuse.

When a date has been made and the boy calls for the girl on time, she should be ready. It isn't proper manners in anyone's etiquette book to keep someone waiting in order not to seem too eager for the date.

CALLING AT THE DOOR

A girl should insist that her date call for her at her house rather than meet her at the corner or at a friend's house. And he should never sit in the car and honk the horn. The extra effort of getting out of the car and coming to the door is an essential courtesy which a girl should expect to receive and the boy expect to give. Anyway, most parents want to meet the boy their daughter is dating. In fact, if at all possible a girl should introduce her date to her parents or to someone who is responsible for her the first time she goes out with him. This is a matter of courtesy to the parents and to the date.

SETTING DEADLINES

Teenagers should not object to parents' setting a time for coming home from a date. If this can be worked out between the girl and her parents (since the time limit is usually set by the girl's parents) with the deadline in keeping with whatever the event is and reasonably in line with the deadlines her friends must meet, so much the better. But setting limits is the responsibility of the parents and this is one place where they must not be overly influenced by what everyone else allows. What others in the group are allowed to do must be considered of course, but in the final analysis family rules must prevail. (See chapter on Children and Teenagers.)

But if there is an unexpected delay, the girl or her date should call home to explain the reason. It *does* happen that sometimes the favorite hamburger spot is overcrowded and an order is delayed. Parents should be courteous in return and allow the extra time—provided this is not just an excuse that is used too regularly.

WEARING SEAT BELTS

What about wearing seat belts? It may be a waste of time to suggest it, but the safe rule is to wear them. It does mean the couple can't sit as close together as they would like. (And driver and passenger in one seat belt doesn't work well!) But wearing seat belts might insure that they are alive to go out on another date.

MANNERS ON A DATE

We have to draw a fine line between a girl being either a clinging vine or too independent. This is true for women of all ages. Of course a girl is able to open a door by herself, and get in and out of a car unaided, and carry her own suitcase, and ring for the elevator herself. And there are times when she may properly do these things even when accompanied by a man. If it is impossible for a man to come around and open the car door for his date to get out, it would be silly for her to sit there helplessly. We always have to use common sense about these things.

But waiting for a man to be courteous helps him to *be* courteous. It gives the girl the feeling of being looked after, and lets the man assume his rightful place of responsibility and leadership in their relationship. This same principle should be carried on through married life.

INVITING A DATE IN

Whether a man is invited into the house after a date or not, he gets out of the car, goes around to open the car door for the girl, and takes her to her door. If she has her own key, he unlocks the door and waits until she is inside before leaving.

If a girl's parents or someone older is not at home, she should not invite her date in and he should not insist on coming in even though they would only sit in the lighted living room and watch television. This propriety is not as strictly observed in the impersonal atmosphere of a city house or apartment as it is in a small town. But it is a wise rule to follow even by the girl who no longer lives at home but has an apartment by herself.

TRAVELING UNCHAPERONED

In fact, any young couple should never put themselves in an awkward position which could be embarrassing because it could be misinterpreted. They should never go overnight anywhere or at any time unless there is adequate supervision. Even an engaged couple should not travel alone overnight unless they use public transportation. What others think of us *is* important and the words in II Corinthians 6:3 are particularly applicable in this matter.

EXCHANGING PRESENTS

Expensive presents between dating couples should neither be given nor accepted. This propriety is often ridiculed but it remains a good one to observe nonetheless. The basic rule is that gifts between teenagers or men and women who are dating, even those who are going steady but are not engaged, should be inexpensive and impersonal. Many teenagers have only a limited amount of money to spend on gifts, which automatically takes care of the problem. But even couples who do have money should observe good taste in the matter. If a girl is offered too expensive or too personal a gift, she should refuse it, even though it is embarrassing to do so. If she needs moral support in the refusal, she can mention her parents' disapproval: "My mother won't let me keep it," which of course should be the truth.

Fortunately there are many gifts which fit the inexpensive, impersonal category. A man would not give a girl expensive jewelry but costume jewelry is all right. Other gifts girls like are gloves, scarves, candy, stationery, books, records, a magazine subscription or perfume. For a man, gloves, scarves, hand-knitted socks, a wallet, books or a magazine subscription (especially a sports or hobby magazine) is a good choice. A New Testament, a devotional book and a Bible in a modern translation are other suggestions.

SIGNING PICTURES

If pictures are exchanged, they are better left unsigned unless the couple is engaged and definitely planning on marriage in the near future. Sentiments have a way of cooling off rapidly, and endearing vows of love written across a picture can be embarrassing.

BEHAVIOR IN PUBLIC

Love is given a false image in these days through movie ads, television programs, books and magazine stories. Even Christian young people become so accustomed to this image that they think of love only in physical terms, and bodily contact becomes for them the evidence of love. This is a true part of love but only a part, and God ordained that physical intimacy belongs only to marriage.

Because emotions are tricky, a young couple in love should avoid being by themselves constantly. They should double-date, or go out with a group, or visit with each other's family frequently. It's wise not to sit too long in a parked car to help avoid falling into a habit of petting which they may not be able to stop when they want to. It is possible *not* to give in to physical desire. A dating couple should respect one another's bodies which are "the temple of the Holy Spirit" (I Corinthians 6:19).

Young people in love often give offense to others by their behavior toward one another in public. For a couple to walk down the street holding hands is one thing. To walk with arms wound around the other and stopping to kiss repeatedly is in extreme bad taste. It doesn't show how much they love one another, but how little they really care for each other's reputation, because it inevitably makes the observer wonder what they do in private.

Even an engaged couple should be discreet in their behavior toward each other, not just because of the impression they make on other people, but because they might find they have been mistaken in their feeling about each other. And while an engagement is a serious step, it is not an irrevocable one. It is much better to break the engagement, or at least postpone the wedding, whenever there is doubt in either person's mind about love for the other.

BECOMING ENGAGED

When a young couple do decide to become engaged, they do not pay as much attention as was formerly done to the formality of asking the girl's father for permission to marry. Yet it is still a polite thing to do as well as being a practical one. Any couple should want the best wishes and the blessing of both sets of parents, and particularly of the girl's parents, who will be paying the larger share of the bills for the wedding. The parents should be the first to know about the engagement.

NOTE OF WELCOME FROM MAN'S MOTHER

The man's mother is supposed to take the initiative in welcoming her future daughter-in-law. This is done in person if they are in the same town, and by phone or letter if they are some distance apart. Even though a close bond of friendship is already established, a girl appreciates a word of loving welcome from her fiancé's parents when she becomes engaged. But of course this is a mutual thing and the bride's parents should also be warm in their acceptance of the man and his family. If the groom's mother doesn't write a note or make a phone call of welcome, it may be she doesn't know she is supposed to. Don't let the fact that a form of etiquette has not been followed cause hurt feelings.

CHOOSING A RING

A ring is not necessary to make an engagement official. Nor, when one is given, does it have to be a diamond even though this is the usual stone that is chosen. Whether the man picks it out himself or takes his fiancée to the jeweler to make the selection with him is entirely a matter of personal preference. If he is quite sure of her taste and knows her ring size, he may choose the ring himself. If he isn't sure, he would be wise to go to a jeweler and ask to see a selection of rings in his price range. Then when he comes in later with his fiancée, the jeweler will show only those rings. This avoids the embarrassment of a girl choosing a ring which costs much more than the man can possibly afford.

A girl should remember that the size of the diamond is not an indication of its quality. She should not be guided in her choice of ring by the size or the value of the one her best friend received. It would be foolish to enter marriage in debt just to have an expensive ring to impress one's friends.

Many couples like to choose the wedding ring at the time the engagement ring is bought so that the rings will match. When the man wears a wedding ring, it should match in design and style the one he chooses for his fiancée.

ANNOUNCING THE ENGAGEMENT

The formal announcement of the engagement is made by the girl's parents. This may be done to close friends in any way the family wishes. An announcement party is nice but certainly is not necessary. Local customs differ in this matter so that if all your friends give a party to announce an engagement, you may want to do so too. Such a party may be only for the family or it may be an open house for one's friends.

But the formal announcement in the newspaper usually follows a set pattern because it gives information to the public. It should be written out exactly as it is to appear in the paper and may read simply:

> Mr. and Mrs. John Charles Smith, 1100 Lake Shore Drive, announce the engagement of their daughter, Miss Mary Louise Smith [or just Mary Louise], to Mr. Richard Jones [or just Richard Jones], son of Mr. and Mrs. John Jones of Atlanta, Georgia.

Additional information may be included, such as the education and/or employment of each, and when the wedding will take place if the date has been set.

The announcement should be typed and mailed or taken to the newspaper office. If it is phoned in, which most newspapers do not want anyway, there is too much chance of mistakes being made. Many newspapers have standard forms to be filled in with this information, and the society editors of newspapers in suburbs and small towns are happy to help in any way they can.

When a picture accompanies the announcement, it should be a black and white glossy, usually 5×7 or 8×10 inches. The man's picture is not included in the engagement announcement even when the announcement appears in his hometown paper. The information for the announcement should be typed on a separate sheet of paper which can be pasted to the back of the picture. If mailed in, the picture should be covered by a piece of cardboard for protection.

If one parent is not living, the engagement announcement reads:

> Mrs. John Charles Smith, 1100 Lake Shore Drive, announces the marriage of her daughter, Mary, to Mr. Richard Jones, son of Mr. and Mrs. John Jones of Atlanta, Georgia. Miss Smith is the daughter of the late Mr. Smith.

If the mother has remarried, the announcement may say:

> Mr. and Mrs. Thomas Brown announce the engagement of her daughter, Miss Mary Louise Smith . . . .

If neither of the girl's parents is living, the announcement may be made by a relative or close friend. Usually the bride-to-be does not make the engagement announcement herself unless she is an older person with no close relatives. Then she may either announce the engagement jointly with her fiancé or else they wait and just announce their marriage. The parents of the man do not ordinarily announce the engagement of their son. The announcement comes from the bride's parents and a copy is sent to the paper of the man's hometown, though probably more information will be added about him.

ANNOUNCING A BROKEN ENGAGEMENT

It is not necessary to announce a broken engagement in the newspaper, for this kind of news usually spreads rapidly by word of mouth. If it is put in the paper it is simply stated:

The engagement of Miss Mary Louise Smith and Mr. Richard Jones has been broken by mutual consent.

RECALLING WEDDING INVITATIONS

However, if invitations have gone out, friends will have to be informed more definitely. If there is time, engraved or printed cards may be sent saying:

> Mr. and Mrs. John Charles Smith
> regret that they must recall
> the invitations to
> their daughter's wedding

or

> Mr. and Mrs. John Charles Smith
> announce that the marriage of
> their daughter Mary
> to
> Mr. Richard Jones
> will not take place

This announcement may also be handwritten or, if the time is really short, people may be notified by telephone or telegram.

RETURNING RING, GIFTS

When an engagement is broken, the girl returns the engagement ring. It really belongs to her legally, but few girls would want to keep it. Any wedding gifts should be returned with a brief note of thanks and explanation. Shower gifts may be kept if the girl wishes, especially if they are not of much monetary value. Of course, if the engagement is broken because of death of the man, the girl would not return the ring to the family unless it were an heirloom which should really belong only to someone in the family. In this case she would also keep any gifts she had received.

ACKNOWLEDGING WEDDING GIFTS

One of the most exciting features for the bride-to-be after the engagement has been announced, is the arrival of gifts from friends. These should be carefully recorded and thank you notes written promptly. The more of these that can be done before the wedding, the less danger there is of someone's gift being forgotten in the excitement. This includes thanking for shower gifts even though these may be nothing more than a set of pot holders or a rolling pin. (See chapter on Entertaining for discussion of showers.)

KEEPING A RECORD OF GIFTS

A girl may devise her own system for keeping track of gifts as long as it is one she can follow. The most practical present she can receive at this time (or get for herself) is a book in which to register gifts. Such a book, which can be purchased at a stationer's store or a gift or department store, has a space for each gift, the giver's name, the store from which it was purchased, often a descriptive space (such as for the color of towels, or glasses), and the date of acknowledgment. In addition, there are pages of gummed numbers which are to be put in an inconspicuous place on each gift as it is opened. These numbers are recorded in the book so that the gifts are not mixed up when thank you notes are written.

REGISTERING AT STORES

Since every girl knows she will receive gifts when her engagement is announced, she and her fiancé would be wise to register at some department and/or jewelry store and at a neighborhood gift shop if there is one. In doing so they select the silver, china and glassware patterns they would like and indicate their preference for other gifts as to color and style. Many brides hesitate to do this because it seems as though they are being greedy and asking for gifts. Actually this is a very sensible system both for them and their friends. Friends are going to buy gifts anyway, and if they know what the young couple would like, they will be able to spend their money wisely by buying something that is really wanted and needed. This also helps to keep the couple from receiving a hodgepodge of unmatched pieces or six toasters and twenty tablecloths.

When the couple is registered at a store those buying gifts ask to see a list of choices and then buy from the list if they want to. When they do, the clerk checks off that item so that someone else does not buy a duplicate. Naturally a young couple should be wise in their choices. If they and their friends are of moderate means, they should not choose silver and china patterns which are extravagantly high just because they will be receiving them as gifts. It's understandable that a woman who has been married twenty-five years and still does not have sterling silver would not want to spend fifty or seventy dollars a place setting for sterling for the daughter of a friend.

BROKEN GIFTS

It is a little difficult to know what to do when a gift arrives in the mail broken. If it was sent directly by the store, you might want to contact the store yourself without mentioning the broken gift to the sender. But if it was mailed by the purchaser, check to see if the package was insured. If it was, it could be returned with a note of regret to the sender who then can contact the post office himself. However, if the package was not insured, how to handle the problem depends on the situation. In a case where the giver might be offended if told that his gift was damaged and you will never see him anyway, you may just have to let it go. A close friend will understand of course, but one never knows how other people will react. If the giver is someone who is apt to visit and wonder where the gift is, naturally you will have to tell him that it arrived broken even if it was due to carelessness on his part.

EXCHANGING GIFTS

Exchanging gifts can also be a touchy matter, and again each case may have to be handled according to the people involved. Ideally each gift should be kept because it represents the thoughtfulness of the one who purchased it, and in later years the gift will bring back memories of that particular friend. However, sometimes a bride receives a half dozen silver candy dishes and no toaster. This may not bother her because she would buy herself the toaster anyway and can always find uses for the candy dishes which she would not buy for herself. Those who give a wedding gift could thoughtfully suggest that they wouldn't mind having it exchanged if it is a duplicate.

DISPLAYING GIFTS

Displaying wedding gifts is optional. If one has room to do it, fine; if not, they don't have to be displayed. If they are displayed, it is usually at the bride's home rather than at the church or wherever the reception is held. One may choose to put out only a few representative gifts on a small table in an easily accessible place. Or, if most of the gifts are displayed, furniture may have to be moved out of a room so that a table can be set up, covered with a pretty cloth, and gifts arranged in any way the bride chooses. If checks are displayed, the amount is covered and only the signature shows. Some people strenuously object to displaying checks. But on the other hand Aunt Matilda might be hurt if her check were not displayed so that people would think she hadn't given anything. This is another one of those situations where one observes good taste and courtesy coupled with common sense and kindness.

In this matter of dating and getting engaged, a couple have more than just themselves to consider, and this is why they must watch their behavior so carefully. A man and woman in love represent to others their families and the kind of training they have had. A Christian couple also represents the Lord Jesus Christ. Scripture says to each of us, "Be thou an example of the believers, in word, in conversation, in charity, in spirit, in faith, in purity" (I Timothy 4:12).

8

WEDDINGS

Marriage is a divinely ordained institution in which a man is commanded to "leave his father and mother" and be "joined unto his wife, and they two shall be one flesh" (Ephesians 5:31). The meaning of the ceremony should be foremost in the thinking of everyone concerned, for it is one in which two people begin a new life. Nothing in the planning should be allowed to take away from the significance of the ceremony.

This subject is of interest to everyone, for each of us at some time is involved in a wedding either as a participant or as a guest. It is an area more fraught with rules and regulations than almost any other. Some of these should be rigidly followed; others may be modified or even set aside completely depending on the individual circumstances.

This chapter will not attempt to cover all the details that are included in planning every kind of wedding, for there are many books available which give such detailed information. But it's well to know that the basic planning remains the same whether one has an elaborate church wedding with ten bridesmaids and an equal number of groomsmen, or a simple home ceremony with only one attendant each.

HOW MUCH TO SPEND

What is spent on a wedding should be within the ability of the bride's family to pay for without going into debt, and not be based on what was spent by the family of the bride's best friend or by the next door neighbors for their daughter. The significance and beauty of a wedding doesn't depend on the price of the bride's dress, the size of the wedding party or the number of guests at the reception. In fact, many young couples who face several years of education before they will be established, prefer to have a less expensive wedding and be given as a gift any other money that might have been spent on it.

A wedding is mainly a religious ceremony, and its basic elements include someone to give the bride away, though this is not essential, an attendant for the bride, a best man, a ring and flowers for the bride, and some kind of reception no matter how small.

PLANNING TIME, PLACE, DATE

When a young couple begin to make their plans, the details of the time and place of the wedding must first be settled. It is the bride who makes these decisions, backed up of course by the groom. Generally the ceremony takes place in the bride's hometown, though there are exceptions to this. A girl who has been away from home, either working or at school, may prefer to have the wedding where more of her friends live. Local custom, weather, the convenience of guests who come from a distance, and the wedding trip plans all affect the decision as to the time of the ceremony.

CONSULTING THE MINISTER

However, you must also ask the advice of the minister who will be marrying you. He has taken part in enough weddings to know where the pitfalls lie. If you have definite ideas of your own regarding the actual ceremony, discuss them with him and think twice before disregarding his advice. A couple has no right to flout the rules of a church or the wishes of the minister if they are asking to be married in the church.

The minister should be consulted to be sure that both he and the church are available for the date you have chosen. Find out from him if there are church rules about decorations in the sanctuary, the use of candles or the taking of pictures. If you are planning to have another minister assist in the ceremony, that should be cleared also. This initial conversation should include premarital counseling or an appointment should be made to have this at a future time.

You will want to consult with the organist about the music and with the custodian, particularly if the reception is to be held at the church.

HEALTH CERTIFICATE, MARRIAGE LICENSE

Almost all states require a certificate of health showing that blood tests have been made, before a marriage license will be issued. The health certificate is good for a limited time only, so it should not be obtained too early. These details can be checked at the county courthouse. The marriage license must be gotten in the state where the marriage takes place.

INVITATION LIST

The invitations are sent out by the bride's family, but the groom's mother is always consulted about those to whom she wishes invitations to go. Both mothers should be realistic in the lists of guests they compile. If the families live in the same town, the two lists would be fairly even, but if the groom's family and friends live some distance away, fewer of them could be expected to attend the wedding.

However, an invitation may be sent even to those who might not be able to attend because of distance or illness. A wedding invitation is sent to show the affection one feels toward one's friends in wanting them to share in the happiness of the day. It is an acknowledgment of friendship, not a request for a gift, even though it is sometimes wrongly interpreted in that way. In fact, those who are invited to the wedding ceremony only, are under no obligation to give a present. If the invitation is to the wedding and/or the reception and one goes, then a gift is in order. If one does not go, the gift is optional.

If the church is small so that only a certain number of guests can be accommodated, then of course the invitation list for the ceremony must be restricted and perhaps more may be invited to the reception.

A wedding invitation should be sent to the minister and his wife, to all members of the wedding party, and to the families of the bride and groom as a memento of the day.

INFORMAL INVITATIONS

It is perfectly correct not to send engraved invita-

tions for a small wedding, but instead to invite friends
either personally, by telephone or by handwritten
notes. The mother of the bride might write:

Dear Katherine,

Mary and Dick are to be married at the First
Presbyterian Church on Friday, April the third, at
five o'clock.

We very much want you to come to the ceremony
and to the reception at our home afterward.

Sincerely,

Mary

There is no set rule for the wording of such informal invitations, nor do they have to be given as far
in advance as do formal invitations.

ENGRAVED INVITATIONS

But if engraved invitations are sent, they follow a
rigid form which the bride-to-be would do well to
follow. It isn't wise to economize too drastically on
engraved invitations since they are not excessively
expensive and they are an important part of the wedding. The difference in cost between good quality and
poor quality paper is small. A soft white with a cream
or ivory tint is a good choice. The stationer or the
store from which you order the invitations will have a
choice of lettering styles and different sizes of invitations to choose from. If you wish, you may also at the
same time order napkins for the wedding reception
and informals or other stationery you will need for
thank you notes.

This is not the place to indulge in anything that is either cute or elaborate. Nor is it the place to defy tradition. Simplicity in the invitation gives a note of elegance which adds to the dignity of the wedding.

Sometimes a couple feels that since this is their ceremony they can do anything they want and send out any kind of invitation they want. And of course they can, if they don't mind the possibility that people will be so busy noting the unusual touches that the real meaning of the ceremony will be lost. Every part of the wedding should be planned carefully so that there are no regrets when one looks back on it in later years.

Since this is primarily a religious ceremony, the invitation requests "the honour of your presence" with honor spelled with a *u*. This is always correct but particularly so when the ceremony takes place in a church. "The pleasure of your company" may be requested for the reception, which is a social time, but not at the marriage ceremony.

An invitation to a church wedding reads:

> Mr. and Mrs. John Charles Smith
> request the honour of your presence
> at the marriage of their daughter
> Mary Louise
> to
> Mr. Richard Thomas Jones
> on Friday, the ninth of October
> One thousand nine hundred and sixty-nine
> at eight o'clock
> First Baptist Church
> Racine, Wisconsin

If the bride's father is a minister, the invitation reads:

The Reverend and Mrs. John Charles Smith
[etc.]

and if the groom is a minister the invitation says:

to
The Reverend Richard Thomas Jones

If the bride's mother is a widow, she sends out the invitations in her name only. If she has remarried, the invitation is worded:

Mr. and Mrs. Robert Brown
request the honour of your presence
at the marriage of her daughter
Mary Louise Smith
[etc.]

A widower sends out the invitations in his name only. If he has remarried, the invitations may indicate that this is his daughter. Or, if the bride has lived closely with her stepmother, the invitations stand as though both were the real parents.

Academic doctorates such as a Ph.D. are not customarily used on wedding invitations, though a theological degree and a physician's title are used.

No RSVP is included when the invitation is to the church ceremony only, since people would not be invited unless there were room for them, and since a church is open to anyone.

It is possible to have invitations done in a raised printing which resembles engraving and is much less expensive. The wording and spacing would remain exactly the same as on those that are engraved.

An invitation to the wedding reception may be included as part of the invitation to the ceremony; if so, it is done in several ways. It may follow the city and state in this way:

> and afterward at the reception
> Heritage Hall

Or it may be put in the lower left of the page below the invitation to the ceremony as follows:

> Reception
> immediately following the ceremony
> at the church

A separate reception card may be enclosed:

> Reception
> immediately following the ceremony
> at
> Park Avenue Hotel
> Lake and Forest Road

If the wedding ceremony is limited to a few guests but many more are invited to the reception, the invitation may read:

> Mr. and Mrs. John Charles Smith
> request the pleasure of your company
> at the wedding reception of their daughter
> Mary Louise
> and
> Mr. Richard Thomas Jones
> on Saturday, the ninth of October
> at half after four
> 1100 Lake Shore Drive
> RSVP

Often a general invitation is put in the church paper or bulletin inviting everyone to the wedding. Generally it says:

> Mr. and Mrs. John Charles Smith invite friends and members of the congregation to the marriage of their daughter, Mary Louise, to Richard Thomas Jones on Friday, October the ninth, at eight o'clock, and to the reception following.

REPLYING TO INVITATIONS

One must always reply to an informal invitation to a wedding, but a reply to a formal invitation to the church ceremony only is not necessary. It isn't strictly necessary to reply to the reception invitation when it is part of the invitation to the marriage ceremony. Neither is it necessary to answer a general invitation to the ceremony and reception. However, one must reply to a personal invitation to the wedding reception. As mentioned in an earlier chapter, invitations are answered in the form in which they were issued. (See chapter on Correspondence.) The answer to the invitation says:

> Mr. and Mrs. William Brown
> accept with pleasure the kind invitation
> [or]
> regret that they are unable to accept
> the kind invitation
> of
> Mr. and Mrs. John Charles Smith
> to their daughter's wedding reception
> Friday, the ninth of October
> Park Avenue Hotel

Such an acceptance or regret is written on a folded sheet of paper and follows this formal wording and spacing. (Again note chapter on Correspondence. Also see chapter on Dating and Engagements for recalling wedding invitations.)

ADDRESSING THE ENVELOPES

Engraved invitations should be mailed from three to four weeks before the wedding. This means that ordinarily they should be ordered at least two months in advance, for it often takes six weeks to make them up. Having them early gives the' bride time to address them without feeling under pressure. This is not a difficult job, but it is time-consuming because of the exactness required. They must be addressed by hand as neatly as possible. It is probably wise to order extra envelopes in case mistakes are made. Naturally the bride does not have to do all the addressing by herself; but most prefer to if they have time, because this is part of the exciting planning and preparation for the wonderful day ahead.

No abbreviations are used in the address on the outer envelope. The name, street address, city and state are written out in full except for the titles Mr., Mrs. or Dr. Numbered streets are spelled out: Second Street, not 2d St; Fourth Avenue, not 4th Ave. A separate invitation should go to each couple and to each guest who is single. For example, Aunt Margaret, though she lives with the family, is sent her own invitation. Grownup children in a family should also receive separate invitations.

The outside of the envelope is addressed either in block or step style:

Mr. and Mrs. John Charles Smith
1510 East Third Avenue
Racine, Wisconsin 53402

and the inside envelope:

Mr. and Mrs. Smith

The children in a family whom you wish to include in the invitation are mentioned on the inner evelope only:

Mr. and Mrs. Smith
Mary and John

If the children's names aren't known to you, you may say:

Mr. and Mrs. Smith and family

A wedding invitation is customarily put into two envelopes. This isn't essential, but the cost of the second envelope is not that much more, and it gives added protection to keep the invitation from being bent. It is put in the inner envelope with the engraving facing the flap of the envelope. The inner envelope is not gummed and is put unsealed into the outer envelope.

The return address should be included on the outside envelope. The post office prefers to have it on the front, but a wedding invitation has a neater appearance if it is on the back flap. The return address may be embossed (not engraved or printed) on the envelope by the printer, which will save a great deal of time for the one addressing the envelopes.

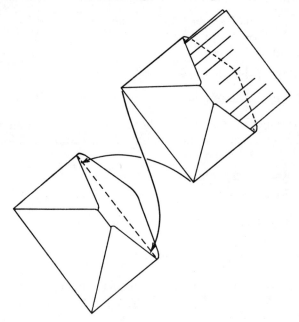

TISSUE SHEETS

The little sheets of tissue which come with the invitations are put there to keep the engraving from being smudged. They may be left in or taken out as one prefers. Either way is correct. Naturally, invitations are always mailed first class so that they may be forwarded if necessary.

Now and then wedding invitations are sent out which give the order of the service and list all the musical numbers, the names of those participating, the responses of the bride and groom, and occasionally responses the audience will make during the service. Sometimes this information is given in bulletin form by the ushers to those attending the wedding.

No etiquette book will recommend this yet no one can say that it is wrong to have a program printed in this way. This is another instance in which those concerned must decide how they want to arrange their marriage service.

WEDDING ANNOUNCEMENTS

Announcements of a wedding are mailed a day or two after the wedding has taken place although, of course, they are addressed earlier. These are not too often sent, but when they are they follow the same form as the invitation:

> Mr. and Mrs. John Charles Smith
> announce the marriage of their daughter
> [or]
> have the honour of announcing
> [etc.]

The couple may announce their own marriage if they wish:

> Miss Mary Louise Smith
> and
> Mr. Richard Thomas Jones
> announce their marriage
> on Friday, the ninth of October
> One thousand nine hundred and sixty-nine
> Atlanta, Georgia

The time of the ceremony is omitted since it has already taken place.

WEDDING EXPENSES

The bride's family bears the largest share of the wedding expenses. These include:

invitations and announcements
photographs
flowers and other church decorations
bride's dress and trousseau
bouquets for bridesmaids
corsages for the mothers and grandmothers (sometimes)
boutonniere for bride's father
food and lodging for bridesmaids
any church fees
fee for organist
reception expenses

The bride (with her family's help if necessary) pays for:

groom's ring
groom's present
her attendants' presents

The groom has a number of expenses also:

bride's engagement and wedding rings
marriage license
minister's fee
bride's bouquet and corsage (which may form the center of the bouquet)
corsages for the mothers and grandmothers (sometimes)

present for bride
attendants' ties and gloves (if worn)
his attendants' food and lodging
bachelor dinner
gifts for his attendants
his boutonniere and those for his attendants and his father
all expenses of wedding trip

The attendants of the bride and groom pay their own transportation expenses to and from the wedding, as do the groom's parents. If formal clothes are to be rented, the ushers take care of the expense themselves. The bridesmaids pay for the dress and shoes they must wear even though it is the bride's right to choose the color and style of dress that will complement her gown. Because this expense may be a hardship, particularly for the girl who is asked to be a bridesmaid several times in one season, a bride should be considerate of her friends and not be extravagant in the price of the dress she chooses. She should also select a style and color each one will look well in.

These expenses are not absolutely fixed. Some of them can either be omitted or adjusted to what each family can afford. The bride and groom do not have to give each other a gift; the bachelor dinner is not a necessity; the ushers' presents may be just the tie each wears; the bride's family may have room to accommodate the attendants and may even be able to afford to pay for the bridesmaids' dresses. All this should be talked over frankly as the plans are made. It is also true that customs differ, and it's best to be guided by what is done locally.

A bride usually chooses her attendants from among her family and close friends, though she might also have a sister of the groom even though she doesn't know her well. It isn't necessary to have attendants in order that the marriage be legal (though most states require two witnesses to sign the marriage license). But both the bride and groom should have at least one attendant each to assist them.

REHEARSAL DINNER

The groom's family often gives the rehearsal dinner, though this is by no means an ironclad rule. It is just as proper for the bride's family to give it or for a relative of either the bride or groom to do so. In fact, it isn't necessary to have such a dinner.

WEDDING RING

The only rules governing the wedding ring are that the bride should have one and that it must be paid for by the groom. Personal tastes in wedding rings vary from generation to generation. The choice is entirely a matter of personal preference and no one style is more correct than another. However, the wedding ring should look well with the engagement ring, and that is why it is wise to choose them at the same time. The advantage of a plain gold or platinum band of medium width is that such a style is never dated and requires no care. If the wedding band is engraved, it is usually on the inside with the initials of the couple and the date of the marriage. The bride puts her engagement ring on her right hand until after the ceremony so that it can be easily slipped back in place after the wedding ring is on her finger.

MAID OF HONOR

Actually, the maid of honor and the best man have important duties to perform in addition to being members of the wedding party and looking decorative. It is the maid of honor who holds the bride's bouquet during the ceremony, takes charge of the groom's ring until the minister asks for it, adjusts the bride's train for the recessional and signs the marriage license as a witness.

BEST MAN

The best man helps the groom at a time when he is understandably nervous. He makes sure the groom has the license, takes charge of the bride's ring until it is needed, puts the minister's fee in an envelope and sees that he receives it, makes sure the groom's suitcase and car are ready for the wedding trip, gets him to the church on time and signs the marriage license. The best man should be the friend the bride and groom can depend on to see that they leave for their wedding trip without any other "friends" delaying them.

WEDDING CLOTHES

The clothes worn by the wedding party are determined by whether the wedding is formal or semi-formal, whether it is in the daytime or in the evening, and whether it is a church, home or civil ceremony. Since it wouldn't be possible to cover all of these adequately, we'll think particularly of a church formal or informal wedding.

Most of us have an immediate picture of the bride as a vision in a white, floor-length gown often with a train, and wearing a veil. But even in this there are variations which depend on the bride's taste.

The bridesmaids' dresses may be long or short, and made of a variety of materials depending on the bride's gown and the time of year. They may all be the same color or each may be different as long as they blend well together. Usually the bridesmaids wear a headdress of some sort, either a hat, ribbons or a veil. The shoes usually match the dress in color, gloves may or may not be worn, and they carry flowers of some kind.

The mothers of the bride and groom wear either long or street-length dresses in colors that complement each other, dressy hats, gloves and corsages. Their shoes often match the color of the dress, though this is not a rule if another color is preferred.

The groom, best man, ushers and fathers dress alike. For an informal daytime wedding they wear an oxford gray stroller with striped trousers, gray waistcoat and a white shirt with a turned-down collar. An informal evening wedding means a white dinner jacket with black tie, black trousers with a satin stripe, and a white shirt with a turned-down collar. A formal daytime wedding requires a cutaway jacket, striped trousers, light waistcoat, wing collar shirt and an ascot. For a formal evening wedding the men wear white tie and tails and matching trousers. Any men's store either has these for rent or will tell you where they may be rented, and can tell you what should be worn when. All the men in the wedding party wear a boutonniere.

Perhaps you don't want to follow this much style.

Nobody will raise eyebrows if you don't. Dinner jackets with black ties or even dark business suits are perfectly acceptable. However, all the men in the wedding party should dress alike. If the groom really wants to go all out in the most formal attire (provided the rest of the wedding warrants it), then the fathers should do the same and not insist on wearing business suits.

REHEARSAL

A rehearsal is a must for this important occasion. No matter how calm the bride and groom may be or how sure of themselves, this is a role neither has played before and they must know what to do and when to do it. This is possible only if they have rehearsed the entire ceremony. Superstition says that a bride should not take part in the rehearsal but only watch as someone takes her place. Most brides feel this is silly and that they can only be sure of themselves during the ceremony if they have actually rehearsed it.

FLOWER GIRL, RING BEARER

Everyone taking part in the wedding should be present for the rehearsal. Even then a little flower girl or ring bearer will be unpredictable just because they are children and can't be depended on to do exactly what they should. A bride might not want to have very young children in her wedding, adorable as they are. It's not selfish of her to want all eyes on her during the ceremony, rather than on a darling little blond three-year-old who smiles entrancingly and waves at all the guests. The darling little blond will have her day later on; let this one belong to the bride.

One point often overlooked in the planning is how to handle the bride's train or long veil when she turns to walk down the aisle. Since she is not wearing her wedding dress for the rehearsal, the maid of honor cannot foresee how much arranging will have to be done. If the bride wears a length of material at the rehearsal in imitation of a train or long veil, a potentially awkward moment during the ceremony may be avoided.

The rehearsal enables those taking part to know when and how to walk down the aisle, how to keep in time with the music, where to stand during the ceremony and how to walk out afterward. The minister will go through the entire service with everyone taking part just as will be done for the ceremony. No words of the actual vows are repeated, although the bride and groom should have a clear understanding with the minister as to what form of ceremony they will use and how the vows will be said.

Because the wedding ceremony is of such a personal, sacred nature, it cannot be dictated by conventional rules. Each couple decides just what belongs in the wedding ceremony to make it distinctively theirs. But it is wise to be careful about innovations either in appearance, in the words of the service or in the music, lest people remember them rather than the sacredness of the occasion.

Generally a sermon on the sanctity of marriage is better given to the bride and groom in private premarital counsel rather than as a part of the ceremony. A sermon to the unsaved is not a part of the wedding ceremony either, because that is not its purpose. The emphasis should be that marriage is the uniting of two people who have first yielded themselves to the Lord.

MARRIAGE VOWS

There is no reason why a couple should not write their own vows if they want to. However, there are certain words that we automatically think of in connection with a wedding because they express the meaning of the marriage ceremony with dignity and beauty. These are found, for example, in the *Book of Common Worship* (of the Presbyterian Church). A young couple should discuss their vows seriously with the minister who will be performing the ceremony.

MUSIC

A similar word of caution should be said with regard to the music that is used for the wedding. Wagner's "Wedding March" from *Lohengrin* for the processional and Mendelssohn's "Wedding March" from *A Midsummer Night's Dream* as the recessional are so traditional that we always associate this music with weddings. But of course these do not have to be used. If other music is chosen, it should be in keeping with the beauty and dignity of the ceremony. Whether the bride and groom choose a soloist, a choir or a trio to sing; whether there is violin, piano or organ music; and whether the musical selections are used before, during or after the taking of the vows, depends on too many factors to adequately discuss briefly. This is part of the plans the bride and groom will discuss with the minister and organist before making a final decision.

CHURCH DECORATIONS

No matter how much advance preparation is made, certain details can't be done until the day of the wedding. One of these is decorating the church. Naturally the bride will have decided weeks earlier what her color scheme will be and how much decoration she wants. She may choose to have a mass of flowers or none at all, but she would do well to ask advice from a florist. Even if she knows exactly what she wants, the florist can give valuable assistance. He knows what flowers will be in season at the time of the wedding. He may even have decorated that particular church a number of times and knows what looks good and what doesn't. The girl who is not sure what flowers to choose either for decorating the church or for the bouquets or other flowers should ask the florist's advice. She should also be frank to say how much she can afford to spend. Some brides prefer to decorate the church themselves, others ask friends to do it for them, and still others ask the florist to do it. Be sure to find out in advance if the florist charges extra for any specialized assistance that he gives.

He can also supply the white canvas runner that is used in the aisle down which the bride walks. If the church does not have the type of candelabra the bride wishes, a florist generally has these available also for rent.

CANDLES

If candles are used, they may be lighted at any time the bride wishes. Some prefer to do this very early before the first guests arrive, when there need be no particular formality about lighting them. Others choose to have them lighted just before the mothers are seated. If so, two people, either ushers or boy or girl relatives of the bride or groom, working in harmony, light the candles, each using a long white candle or a candlelighter. One might also use electric candelabra or the newer candles which have a liquid in them. These are safer although they do not give as soft a glow.

Sometimes the bride and groom each take a lighted candle and jointly light one tall candle to symbolize the uniting of their lives. This is usually done at an appropriate point after the marriage vows have been taken.

SEATING GUESTS

The ushers are responsible for seating guests as they arrive. The one who is most familiar with the guests usually has charge of the middle aisle assisted by other ushers. The usher offers his right arm to a woman guest and escorts her to a place, with the husband and the rest of the family following. In the case of several women coming together, the usher escorts just one and the rest follow. The bride's side of the church is to the left of the aisle, the groom's to the right (facing the front of the sanctuary), and relatives and close friends of each are seated accordingly. However, if there are many less friends and relatives of the groom because they live too far to come, guests should be seated more or less evenly to avoid an unbalanced appearance.

SEATING MOTHERS

The groom's mother is taken by an usher to her place in a front pew on the right, with the groom's father following. She is seated just before the bride's mother, who comes in a few minutes before the ceremony begins. No one should be seated by an usher after she comes in; any late arrivals must find seats in back rows. As soon as the bride's mother is seated, two ushers come down the aisle to unroll the white aisle canvas, if one is used, which is already in place at the front of the church.

PROCESSIONAL

The groom and best man usually wait with the minister in the study or some room off the sanctuary. They go into the sanctuary when the organist begins the music which indicates that the rest of the bridal party is ready to enter, and they wait at the front of the church to the left of the minister facing the guests. Sometimes the ushers wait with them and come in at the same time. Sometimes they precede the bridesmaids down the aisle, and sometimes the ushers and bridesmaids are paired together to come down the aisle. The junior bridesmaid, if there is one, walks first, then the ushers and bridesmaids or bridesmaids only, the maid or matron of honor, the flower girl, the ring bearer, and finally the bride who may be either on the right or the left arm of her father.

It is the bride's mother who indicates whether guests

are to remain seated or to rise during the ceremony. If they are to stand, she rises when the first notes of the wedding march indicate that the bride has started down the aisle. Either way is correct. It is often preferable for guests to remain seated so that all may see better.

CEREMONY

The father stands with his daughter during the ceremony until the minister asks, "Who giveth this woman to be married to this man?" After answering, "I do" or "Her mother and I do," he relinquishes his daughter to the groom (who moves to her side), and takes his place beside his wife. If the bride's father is a minister and is to perform the rest of the ceremony, instead of sitting down he steps into place beside the assisting minister. This should be rehearsed so that it is done smoothly.

The bridal party then forms in position as they have rehearsed. The arrangement will depend on the number of attendants and the space. Only the maid or matron of honor and best man stand close to the bride and groom. Any balanced arrangement that looks nice may be used, either having bridesmaids and ushers on either side or pairing them. A frequently used arrangement is this:

Minister

Bride   Groom

Maid of Honor   Best Man

Bridesmaid   Usher

Bridesmaid   Usher

Bridesmaid   Usher

Before the rings are exchanged, the bride hands her bouquet to the maid of honor who holds it until the end of the ceremony.

RECESSIONAL

After the minister has pronounced the couple husband and wife, the groom lifts the face veil and kisses his bride, then they turn to face the guests. It is customary in some places for the minister to say, "It is my pleasure to introduce to you Mr. and Mrs. Richard Jones." This gives the maid of honor a moment to arrange the bride's train before she starts down the aisle on her husband's right arm. The bridesmaids either come down the aisle paired off with the ushers or precede them down the aisle. One usher returns immediately to escort the bride's mother out first, and another usher escorts the groom's mother, followed in each case by the father. Other guests are then free to leave. Often the ushers allow only one row at a time to leave, starting at the front, to avoid a crush in the church vestibule, particularly if the reception is held at the church. If there is no reception or only a small one for family and close friends, the bride and groom should wait in the narthex or vestibule so that guests may greet them.

RECEIVING LINE

The receiving line at the reception ordinarily is composed of the bride and groom, the mothers and the bridesmaids. The fathers may also have a place but not the ushers. The usual order is for the bride's mother to stand first, then the groom's father, the groom's mother, the bride's father, the bride, the groom, the maid of honor and the bridesmaids. The reason the bride's mother stands first is that usually more of the guests are known to her and she, as the hostess, introduces them to the groom's parents. However, this order need not be rigidly adhered to if those concerned wish to stand in some other arrangement.

This is true also of some of the other wedding procedures. There are certain conventions or traditions to follow as in all relationships of life. But if following them absolutely causes a problem for someone, or if circumstances are such that tradition simply can't be followed, don't feel that therefore there can't be a wedding. A bride's happiness should never be spoiled by an inflexible rule. It won't matter if all the plans can't be exactly like the book; most of the guests won't care and many won't know, as long as dignity and simplicity and reverence prevail throughout the wedding.

The reception line is not the time or place for guests to have an extended conversation with the bride and groom. It is enough just to express a wish for their happiness. A guest must remember not to congratulate the bride. She is given the guest's best wishes; it is the groom who receives the congratulations. A minor point but an important one.

TAKING PICTURES

No matter how carefully the bride plans, there will inevitably be a delay in getting the reception started, even if it is held at the church. Part of the delay is due to the need of having the formal posed group pictures taken. If it can be arranged, the bride's formal picture should be taken several days before the wedding. This often isn't possible, and so it and the group pictures must be taken at the church. Sometimes it is more convenient for the wedding party to go back to the church sanctuary for the pictures after all the guests have been escorted out; other times it is better to greet the guests first and then return for the pictures. More and more brides are having candid pictures taken and fewer posed photographs. However, a photographer must be careful not to intrude during the ceremony. All one can do is to plan this in the best way possible and then not worry if there is a delay. Most guests are understanding and willing to wait a little while if it is necessary.

RECEPTION

The wedding reception may be an elaborate sit-down meal or simply wedding cake and a beverage. It may be catered professionally or be in charge of friends. This is a matter of personal preference entirely and there is no rule that says it must be one way or the other.

When a meal is served, there is usually a bridal table at which the bride and groom and their attendants sit. The rest of the guests may either be seated at other tables or served buffet style. The wedding cake is the centerpiece on the bridal table and is not cut until after the meal.

WEDDING CAKE

At a simpler reception the wedding cake is also the

centerpiece on the refreshment table. It may be the only food served, or there may also be cookies, tiny sandwiches, nuts and mints, as well as coffee, tea and/or punch. Cutting the cake presents a little more of a problem at this kind of reception. Everyone wants to see it cut of course, and the bride must either wait to cut it after all the guests have come into the room where the reception is held and then form the receiving line, or else wait until everyone has gone through the line before cutting the cake. Either way there is a delay but most people don't mind waiting. Some brides have a separate table set up where someone serves punch to those who have gone through the receiving line.

The cake usually is a tiered one with white icing. The bride and groom together cut a slice from a lower layer since the top layer is traditionally removed for the bridal couple to keep. Many couples keep it frozen until the first anniversary. A thoughtful friend might buy a silver cake knife as a wedding gift and have it engraved with the couple's names and the date of the wedding. After the first slice has been cut and the bride and groom have given each other a bite, someone else takes over to cut the rest and serve the guests. In some places it is customary to have a groom's cake also, which is a rich fruitcake. This is not served at the reception. Instead, a slice of cake is boxed or wrapped in waxed paper for each guest to take home.

Close friends of the bride often assist in serving at the reception. Several preside at the table, one has the responsibility of the guest book, another is in charge of gifts that are brought to the wedding.

Wedding gifts ought to be sent to the bride's home and not brought to the church, but there are always reasons why some cannot do this. Before the wedding the gifts are addressed to the bride alone even by friends of the groom who do not know her. After the wedding, gifts are addressed to them both.

THROWING THE BRIDE'S BOUQUET

The bride and groom may either slip out of the reception quietly or say good-bye to everyone before leaving. Sometimes they are able to change into traveling clothes at the church; sometimes they return to the bride's home for this. Whatever they do, the guests who are still at the reception will want to see the bride throw her bouquet and have a chance to shower the couple with rice (though this should be checked in advance with the church caretaker). Whoever catches the bride's bouquet keeps it of course. Usually the bride aims it at the one she wants to have it. If there is an elderly relative who could not attend the wedding, the bouquet could be given to her. And of course the bride can keep it herself if she wants to.

MILITARY WEDDINGS

There are other types of weddings to which this basic planning can be applied. The procedure for a military wedding follows special rules of protocol and any couple planning such a wedding should consult someone who knows the details. In brief, if the bride is a daughter of a military person and is having a military wedding, it is usual to ask the chaplain of her father's post to perform the ceremony. If she is from a civilian family but is having a military wedding, she may ask her own minister or the groom's chaplain. The bride's attendants are dressed as for a civilian wedding, but the groom's attendants are usually fellow officers who wear their uniforms. It is not necessary of course for a military man to have a military wedding.

CIVIL CEREMONY

A civil ceremony can be as dignified and reverent as a church wedding. The bride would wear a suit or a street-length dress, a hat, and gloves which are removed just before the ceremony. Usually she would wear a corsage rather than carry a bouquet. The groom would wear a business suit. When the ceremony is performed by a justice of the peace, there is usually a set fee.

SECOND MARRIAGES

A widow may have a church ceremony for her second marriage although she does not wear white and does not have a veil. If it is the groom's second marriage, this does not affect the bride's plans provided she is marrying for the first time. Of course if either is divorced this may prevent them from having a church wedding. Engraved invitations are not sent for a second marriage although engraved announcements may be.

NEWSPAPER WRITE-UP

If the bride wants a description of her wedding in the paper, she should check in advance to see what the deadline is for submitting information. This is particularly important if a picture is to accompany the story. To be sure it is accurate, the bride should take time before the wedding to write out the story, giving details of her dress, the attendants, out-of-town guests and any other information she wants included.

WEDDING ANNIVERSARY GIFTS

It is often difficult to know what to give as a gift for a wedding anniversary. Usually only the couple themselves and their immediate families are interested in the yearly anniversary, at least until the twenty-fifth is reached. But here is a basic list which is fairly standard:

1st year—paper or plastics
2d year—cotton
3d year—leather
4th year—silk or linen
5th year—wood
6th year—iron
7th year—wool or copper
8th year—bronze, electrical appliances
9th year—pottery
10th year—tin or aluminum
11th year—steel
12th year—linen
13th year—lace
14th year—ivory
15th year—crystal
20th year—china
25th year—silver
30th year—pearls

35th year—coral or jade
40th year—ruby
45th year—sapphire
50th year—gold
55th year—emerald
60th-75th—diamond

However, there is no reason this list has to be followed except for the twenty-fifth and fiftieth anniversaries. If a young couple received very little silver or china when they were married, any anniversary is a good time for family and friends to give them additional place settings.

Should the phrase "please omit gifts" be included on an invitation to a twenty-fifth or fiftieth anniversary? The answer depends on the circumstances. Usually the party is given by friends of the couple so they are not asking for gifts for themselves. Those invited to such a happy occasion want to honor the couple in some way and like to show their friendship by bringing a gift. If gifts are brought by some and not by others, none of them are opened until after the guests have left.

The marriage of two people in itself is a beautiful and sacred event, but its meaning becomes even deeper when we remember that in the Scripture marriage is used as an illustration of the relationship that exists between Christ and the church: "Therefore as the church is subject unto Christ, so let the wives be to their own husbands in every thing. Husbands, love your wives, even as Christ also loved the church, and gave himself for it" (Ephesians 5:24-25).

9

FUNERALS

Not only does God tell us to rejoice with others, He also commands that we "weep with them that weep" (Romans 12:15). Often we neglect to show the interest and sympathy we really feel for those in sorrow because we are not sure what to say or do. It is always better to express sympathy, even though awkwardly, than not to say anything at all. Yet there are certain proprieties to observe in connection with a funeral.

This is another experience in life which comes to each of us at some time, and it is one for which we are seldom prepared. It is a time when even those who have rarely attended church are generally more tender toward spiritual matters. But it is also a time when very practical matters must be decided suddenly by those who are bereaved. Someone must be in charge to make the arrangements for the funeral with as little pain as possible to those who are most deeply bereaved.

BUSINESS DETAILS

There are business details that must be handled in connection with a funeral. Sometimes bank accounts are frozen immediately on the death of the one to whom the account belonged and funds cannot be withdrawn until a court order is obtained. This sometimes takes months. If there is a will or other legal papers, they must be seen to. A burial plot may have to be purchased. If it is a woman who is bereaved, she should have someone to whom she can turn for advice in these matters.

SELECTING THE COFFIN

One of the most important of the business details and one that must be decided immediately is what kind of funeral the family wants. This includes selecting the coffin. A bereaved person quite rightly wants to show his respect and love for the one who has died, and he often mistakenly thinks this means he must choose an expensive casket. But this isn't necessary. Often a very simple coffin is chosen even by those who can well afford an expensive one. Certainly it is foolish to plunge into debt those who remain in order to give the one who has died an elaborate funeral. This may really be fear of what others will think rather than an evidence of respect for the loved one.

In facing this practical matter and making this decision, the Christian will be helped as he remembers that though the human body decays and crumbles when it is buried, there will be a day when "the trumpet shall sound, and the dead shall be raised incorruptible, and we shall be changed" (I Corinthians 15:52). The coffin that is chosen is only a temporary resting place.

CONSULTING THE MINISTER AND FUNERAL DIRECTOR

If death occurs at some place other than a hospital, either the family doctor or the coroner is called to determine the cause of death. Then a minister and the funeral director are consulted. The funeral director must have a death certificate signed by a doctor in order to move the body to the funeral home. He will also have to be given clothes to dress the body. These should be the kind the person would ordinarily wear to church.

PAID DEATH NOTICE

The funeral director is generally the one who puts the paid death notice in the paper, so he will need information about the person. However, the family may do this if they wish, and the information may be phoned in. Such a notice is put in the paper at regular space rates and, if done by the funeral director, is included in the expenses of the funeral. The usual form of the notice is:

> Smith—John Charles, June 11, beloved husband of Mary Brown Smith and father of Mary Louise, Susan and Richard. Funeral at Roberts Funeral Home (give address if necessary), Friday, June 14, at 2:00 P.M. Visitation Thursday, 7:00 to 9:00 P.M. Burial at Green Haven Cemetery.

The age of the person is not given in the paid death notice except in the case of children. A picture is never included with such a notice.

If the family wishes to have further information put in the paper, it is written up and taken or mailed to the newspaper office just as for any news release, and there is no charge for this. Usually a picture is not included in an obituary unless the person is very well known.

RESPECTING FAMILY WISHES

Sometimes phrases like "funeral private" or "interment private" are used instead of the information as to where the funeral service or burial will be held. People should respect the wishes of the family in this and none but relatives should attend a private funeral. On the other hand anyone, even strangers, may go to a public funeral, especially when it is in a church. Whether children should attend is a question only the individual family can decide.

SENDING FLOWERS

If a death notice asks that flowers be omitted, friends should be very careful to observe the family wishes in this, for the request would not be made without a reason. Flowers are never sent to an orthodox Jewish funeral. If they are sent to a funeral in a Catholic church, they would probably not be taken into the church, since floral arrangements at the altar are always limited. One could send flowers to the local hospital in the name of the deceased person and write a note to the family indicating that this had been done. If the family asks that contributions be made to a charity or to a mission in lieu of flowers and you do so, the organization will notify the family that you have contributed but will not mention the amount that was given.

When flowers are sent, they are usually ordered from the florist so that they will arrive on the day of the funeral. However, it is well to have the flowers at the funeral home by the time of the visitation. A visiting card or just a plain white card supplied by the florist is signed and then addressed to:

> The funeral of Mr. John Charles Smith
> First Presbyterian Church
> Funeral 2:00 P.M., Friday

If the flowers are sent to the funeral home, it isn't necessary to put on the time of the service since those in charge know it. The florist will deliver the flowers.

VISITATION

When the family has decided upon the hours for visitation, this information is made known to friends, sometimes in the death notice, and people are free to come to the funeral home during the hours set. Even though the service will be held in the church, the visitation is usually at the funeral home. The casket is open and members of the family or representatives of them are there to receive the expressions of sympathy from friends. One signs the register, speaks to the family and leaves. It isn't necessary to stay long unless it is obvious that the family want you to keep them company. The way the register is signed depends to some extent on how close you are to the family. "John and Mary Smith" is fine if you know the family well. If you don't, the name may not mean anything to them; "Mr. and Mrs. John Charles Smith" is always an acceptable way to sign the register.

SERVICE IN A CHURCH

The funeral service is seldom held at home, but is either at a church or a funeral home. This is a decision the family makes. If the one who has died was active in his church and many people probably will attend the service, then it is usual to have it in the church.

It is the family's decision as to whether the casket is left open or is closed during the service. It is always in place at the front of the church before the family and friends arrive. The family generally come in from a side room, if there is one, or else walk down the aisle to the right-hand front pew.

If the casket is open, friends may go up to see the body before finding a place to sit. It isn't necessary to have ushers for a funeral service, though they are helpful if a large crowd attends.

PALLBEARERS

The pallbearers walk in slowly two by two after the family has entered and sit in the left front row. These are usually six or eight men who in a sense are honorary because they ordinarily do not carry the casket very far. They do help lift it into the hearse and then carry it from the hearse to the gravesite at the cemetery. The pallbearers are chosen from among the friends of the deceased and the family should be represented in some way. It is very seldom that one would refuse to be a pallbearer if asked.

The minister and the family decide what is said during the service and what music is played or sung.

In some communities, the casket is wheeled down the aisle after the service with the pallbearers and family following. In others, particularly when the casket has remained open during the service, all except close relatives file past to pay their respects to the deceased and then leave immediately. A member of the family may then draw up the slumber robe, after which all leave for the cemetery.

SERVICE AT A FUNERAL HOME

If the service is held at the funeral home, the arrangements are handled professionally though according to the family's wishes. One advantage in having the service in the funeral home is that if fewer friends are able to attend, they do not seem as lost as they would in a large church. Also there is often an adjoining room where the family may sit during the service so that their grief is not exposed so openly to public view. Those attending the service come forward after it is over to view the body and then go immediately outside so that the family and the minister have a few moments alone with the loved one before the casket is closed. Generally the friends do not leave until the casket has been brought out and the family are in their cars.

PROCESSION TO CEMETERY

Anyone may go to the cemetery unless it has been stated that the burial is private. The pallbearers follow the hearse in one car and the immediate family follows in another. All the cars keep together in a slow procession. This is made easier if the car lights are turned on in the daytime so that other drivers recognize that it is a funeral procession.

GRAVESIDE SERVICE

The committal service at the cemetery is always brief. The grave site is usually already prepared, often with an awning over the grave and a few chairs for the family.

Others who have come, stand while the minister reads a brief Scripture portion and offers prayer. The casket is not lowered into the ground until after the family and friends have left. Most of the flowers are taken to the cemetery and put on top of the grave after it is covered. If the family wishes, some of the flowers may be sent to hospitals for use in the wards.

MEMORIAL SERVICE

If the funeral is private or is held in another city, a memorial service may be held a few weeks after the burial. This is usually held in a church with a brief eulogy by the minister and/or a friend. There is either opportunity for friends to speak to the family there, or an announcement is made that the family will meet friends at home.

CLOTHES FOR A FUNERAL

People attending a funeral often wear dark or conservative colors though it is not necessary to wear black. Custom is no longer rigid about those in mourning wearing black. This is an individual matter. No one should judge one who mourns either by his clothing or by his behavior because everyone shows his grief differently. Some people must go into temporary seclusion in order to recover themselves. Others must have people around them constantly. For most, resuming a normal life as early as possible is one of the best ways to recover from the loss. It is best for children to return to school or take up their normal activities immediately.

FEES

There are certain fees in addition to those paid to the funeral director, which vary with individual circumstances. The organist usually receives about fifteen dollars and perhaps more if a great deal of music is played. If there is a soloist, his fee is in proportion to the one given the organist. Even if these are family friends, one should not assume that their services are free. If they do not wish to keep the money for themselves, they may do with it as they wish, but it should be given to them. The minister is given a fee also. If he is one's own minister, he may prefer that the money be given to the church. The money, either in check or cash, is put in an envelope with a handwritten note asking that he do what he wants with it. The amount depends on the size of the funeral, how much the family can afford, and whether they are members of the church. These fees may be handled by the family directly, or the funeral director will see that they are taken care of.

SHOWING SYMPATHY

There is always a rush of sympathy when one hears of the death of a friend or the close relative of a friend. Usually one should follow one's first instinctive desire to do something for the family. It is better not to make a phone call or to call personally at the home immediately, unless it is to leave food. But one should write a note, or offer to take small children temporarily, or run errands or send in food. One should certainly do something for a friend who has lost a loved one. The Lord Jesus went to the home of Mary and Martha and shared their grief, weeping with them (John 11:33-35).

It is customary in many places for friends to provide food for the family after the funeral service either at their house or at the church. We often have the idea that people want to be alone with their grief and this is true of course. But if relatives and friends can gather together in a time of sorrow and express their feelings, there is a therapeutic value which is helpful to the bereaved. Even laughter at a time like this is not out of place, for it relieves what might otherwise be unbearable emotions. Eating together and talking after a funeral service help to lessen the burden of grief. There is also the practical benefit to the family of not having to be responsible for feeding relatives and friends who have come from a distance.

SYMPATHY CARDS

There are many sympathy cards to choose from to send to a friend in sorrow, though just a card with a signed name is rather cold comfort. It is better to write a few lines expressing one's personal sentiments. (See chapter on Correspondence.)

ACKNOWLEDGING FLOWERS AND FOOD

The same principle should be followed in answering expressions of sympathy. The funeral director will provide printed cards which one may use. However, if one takes time to acknowledge expressions of sympathy at all, it should be done with more than just one's name on the bottom of an already printed card. The funeral director will keep the cards that come with the flowers and make a note of what kind they are. One ought to acknowledge flowers that are sent: "Thank you so much for the spray of white roses which we know expressed your thoughts for us." Also one should thank those who send food or help in other specific ways.

But to answer personally every card or note of sympathy that comes is sometimes impossible, particularly when there are many sent. Real friends will not mind if the bereaved person finds it impossible to answer even within the six-week time limit. Friends express their sympathy and understanding for another's grief without expecting acknowledgment.

CHRISTIAN RESPONSE TO DEATH

Death is an experience we all dread and yet one we know is inevitable. But even in it the Christian can exclaim, "Blessed be God, even the Father of our Lord Jesus Christ, the Father of mercies, and the God of all comfort; who comforteth us in all our tribulation, that we may be able to comfort them which are in any trouble, by the comfort wherewith we ourselves are comforted of God" (II Corinthians 1:3-4).

10

CHILDREN AND TEENAGERS

Impoliteness and even rudeness in a child is often excused by an offhand, "He's only a child; he'll grow out of it." But the Scripture reminds us that "even a child is known by his doings, whether his work be pure, and whether it be right" (Proverbs 20:11). No one inherits good manners and a gracious spirit. These must be taught by parents who are conscious of their responsibility to "train up a child in the way he should go" (Proverbs 22:6).

GOOD MANNERS BY EXAMPLE

Children can be given a head start in good manners by the example of their parents. In etiquette rules, as in every other area of life, it is easier to establish good habits than it is to break bad ones. But to teach courteous behavior requires patience, constant repetition and consistency on the part of parents. It means that good manners must be a part of daily living in the home. The father who hunches over his food, is rude to his wife and grabs the newspaper first, will instill that kind of behavior in his son. The mother who throws the silverware on the table any old way makes it hard for the daughter to learn proper table setting. Parents who never say please and thank you to their children can't expect politeness in return.

MANNERS AND SPIRITUAL GROWTH

One goal of teaching good manners is to make the child acceptable in society. The Christian parent adds another dimension when he combines good manners with the spiritual growth of his child. Teaching personal cleanliness should be coupled with the scriptural truth that the child is the temple of God and his body is not his own. Helping him share his toys implies the greater responsibility of sharing with others the good news of Jesus Christ. Training him to clean his room and take care of his belongings can focus his thinking on the orderliness of God in the universe. Teaching him politeness instills the larger truth that God wants His children to be thoughtful of others and to give thanks in everything (I Thessalonians 5:18).

What manners then should children be taught? Exactly those they must have when they become adults. Some of these can't be quickly put on like candy-coating; they must simply be learned and ingrained. We should set as high a standard as possible for the age of the child, and work toward reaching it.

TABLE MANNERS FOR CHILDREN

A child must learn how to hold a pencil when he writes, a boy to hold a baseball bat, a violinist to hold his bow correctly. Why should there not also be training in how to hold silverware, how to break bread before eating it, how to eat soup quietly? Naturally there are times when allowances are made. Children at a birthday supper are going to feel more relaxed than they would at a dinner where there are adult guests. This is all right if it is understood that such times are the exception and not the rule.

Not much can be accomplished in table manners until a child is old enough to sit by himself and hold a spoon to feed himself reasonably well. But when that age is reached, a child can begin to learn how to hold a knife and fork, not to take too large a mouthful of food at once, not to talk with food in his mouth, not to eat noisily or chew with his mouth open. He should learn to sit straight on a chair and not play with silverware and dishes.

Parents do have to be reasonable in their demands and not expect a child to be comfortable very long on a chair that is too big for him or listen in silence to adult conversation from which he is excluded. Some parents feed their children early so they can enjoy their own meal without interruption, but this is not training them for times when they will have to eat with adults. Young children should be expected to sit quietly with the family until they have finished their meal and then they should be excused. The older they get, the longer they should be expected to stay at the table. No one should go away from the table without asking to be excused.

Parents are responsible for the atmosphere of the meal. This means they must put aside their own interests and concerns in order to make meals an enjoyable part of the day. This will be a big factor in establishing good manners.

The dinner table is not the place for parents to nag and scold or for mother to report on all the misbehavior of the day. Parents should refrain from a barrage of corrections during a meal, giving only those that are necessary. There should be no comments on the food if it is not liked; this is a place where parental example is especially important. Children who have happy memories of the family dinner table will in turn be good company when they are on their own, and will be apt to have a happy dinner table in their own home.

A Christian family especially, which has asked God's blessing on the food and thanked Him for His care through the day, should not then degenerate into a bickering, faultfinding group. Coming to family meals should be considered a privilege. No one has the right to annoy others by boorish behavior or an unpleasant appearance whether he be child or adult, family member or guest.

Neatness at the table should be required from the very beginning. The mother who takes time to wash her baby's hands before spoon-feeding him is beginning a habit which she will later transfer to him as his responsibility. Dirt and children have a mutual attraction and there is a time and place for the combination. But at the table everyone must have clean hands and face and combed hair.

PRACTICE FOR COMPANY MEALS

Help children know what to do when they later will be at a more formal banquet by occasionally serving a meal that requires the use of three forks and several spoons. It doesn't matter if they are stainless steel; they are used in the same way and in the same order as sterling. Take children to a restaurant now and then so that both boys and girls have practice in eating out before going on that first important date. Give a young son practice in seating his mother or sister so that he will feel at ease when this is necessary later.

OTHER SOCIAL GRACES

The other social graces that children should learn are those they will need to know and practice when they are grown. These include knowing how to greet people politely; to answer when spoken to and to shake hands; to say, "Yes, thank you" or "No, thank you" instead of just yes or no; to let older people precede them through a door; not to talk about private matters in public; to show respect for other people's opinions, property and privacy; to write thank you notes. The child who has never been taught these manners will not do them automatically when he is grown though he may have to learn them the hard way.

These manners do not come naturally to a child. They must be taught before they are needed, which means that they must be practiced at home. Even then the practice does not become automatic for a long time and patient repetition is necessary.

A child may learn to greet his mother when she plays at being a visitor, and yet be so overwhelmed by shyness when a real visitor comes to the door that he hides behind his mother or buries his head in her lap. It does no good for his mother to haul him out and insist on his shaking hands, or insist that he tell the visitor his name or say thank you for a gift. This only embarrasses everyone and doesn't make it easier for him to do it right the next time. It is best to let it go for that time and later tell him quietly and lovingly what he should do the next time.

The art of conversation should be developed early in life. If children are taught to share their ideas by parents who listen sympathetically, and then are taught to listen in turn, they will be well on the way to being good conversationalists when they become adults. It is true that children must be taught not to interrupt a conversation, but this involves courtesy on the parents' part as well. Many parents scold their children for interrupting but think nothing of barging into the conversation of their children. Perhaps if parents treated their children as people, some of the communication gap between the generations would be bridged. Children who are included in conversations, especially at the dinner table, and spoken to in reasonable, pleasant tones by parents who expect the same kind of treatment in return, find it less necessary to misbehave in order to get attention.

Too often parents have a double standard in their treatment of guests and children. The guest whose cup of coffee spills over the tablecloth is reassured that it is not important; the child whose glass of milk tips over is scolded for his carelessness. Children are quick to note this discrepancy.

CHILDREN'S DRESS

Parents must begin very early to teach children to

dress properly. At some times playclothes are right, at others they are not; it is as simple as that. The clothing problem with young children is not so much one of battling over styles as it is battling over clean versus dirty clothes. Childhood is not too soon to begin to instill a sense of pride in personal appearance. It is in this area as children grow older that the plea "But everyone else does" comes into full sway. Parents should allow as much conformity to the dress of friends and community standards as possible without throwing out their own ideas of what is right. "Be not conformed to this world" is not an easy rule for anyone to live by, but that does not mean that it should therefore be ignored.

LEARNING RESPECT FOR OTHERS

Children must learn respect for other people at a very early age. They should learn while very young not to laugh at someone else either for his appearance, his opinions or his mistakes. They must learn respect for another's privacy, which includes not opening someone else's mail or listening in on phone conversations or entering a closed room without knocking on the door. They should be taught that respecting another's property refers not just to things but to another's rights. This has to begin at home. The child who is allowed to take his brother's toys without asking will not see why he can't do the same to a friend. The child who grows up thinking the other family members are there for his convenience will go out into society with that false premise.

The home belongs to the child in the sense that he is

a part of it; but he must learn that he is only a part and that there are others to consider. Children need to be trained in hospitality, but it is not always convenient for a mother to have a child's friend stay for a meal. There should be an understanding about when this can be done, and when an agreement is reached it should be held to consistently. If it is understood that a spontaneous lunch invitation may be given at any time because it simply means getting out another soup bowl and spreading another peanut butter and jelly sandwich, that is fine. But when it is agreed that a dinner or an overnight invitation must be checked out before it is offered, then parents must not make exceptions. All of this is part of training in good manners.

Perhaps this is where the basic rule of children's respect for elders comes most sharply into focus and the need for it is seen most clearly. Parents can never be buddies to their children and still do the job God intended them to do. Friends, yes, but not equals, for there is an adult-child relationship set by God. If children can learn to respect their parents' experience, good judgment and wisdom, it will make it easier for them to live with rules they do not agree with.

MANNERS IN ADOLESCENCE

If this respect has been ingrained in childhood, and the parents have in turn kept a warm, loving relationship with their children, the adolescent years will not be so frightening and full of home problems. It is true that sometimes years of good manners seem to be lost almost overnight because of the physical changes of adolescence which affect the emotional and social aspects of life.

But good manners learned in childhood are seldom permanently lost. The young person who learned as a child to write thank you notes and to keep his elbows off the table while eating, will usually continue to do so as a matter of habit. Those who have learned and practiced the rules of introduction as children will find the right phrases coming naturally to their lips though perhaps a little less formally than they were taught.

Parents must remember too that some apparent teenage bad manners are partly due to the age. Since they are no longer children, they are expected to behave as adults when they have not had enough experience to know automatically what is correct and what isn't. Because adolescence is an age when a young person is highly self-conscious and easily embarrassed, he is not sure of himself and so is often awkward and seemingly rude. It is also a time of wanting to be independent from parental rules and this sometimes includes independence from good manners.

This is where the foundations laid in childhood and the communication or lack of it between parents and children are evident. Whether the rules are laid down arbitrarily or whether a mutual understanding is reached between parents and children, there are standards of behavior which teenagers should observe simply because they are members of society and because they belong to a family unit. These are the same standards of personal appearance and general behavior which were outlined in the first chapter and which apply to everyone. Every person regardless of his age must have clean skin, teeth, hair and clothes and be polite to others.

As children become teenagers they and their parents face the anguish and the fun of dating. This is another important area where parents dare not abdicate their responsibility for their young people. (See chapter on Dating and Engagements.)

TEENAGE DRESS

Adolescence is an age when a certain kind of sloppiness and a slavish following of current fads is almost a religion. This is all right as long as correct dress is worn when and where it should be. Some patterns of clothing are set by the family, school and community while others are set by teenage fashions, and conflicts sometimes arise between the two. During vacations, around the house, out camping, and other times when there is no particular reason to dress up, rules should be relaxed. But when eating in a restaurant, going to school and church, coming to the dinner table, or anyplace where other people see you, you can't wear anything you want. This is not a double standard that applies only to teens; it is for everyone. No man or boy should come to the dinner table in bare feet and without a shirt.

It isn't possible in a book on etiquette to go into detail on what is or isn't correct in styles because it would be out of date before the book was published. But avoiding extremes in clothing is not being cowardly, only sensible.

CLOTHING ALLOWANCE

Parents can develop good clothes sense in their young people by letting them help select their clothes and giving them direction on what is becoming to them. Parents should be less critical about fads and allow them where possible, because many of them are harmless and change rapidly. Nothing can make a young person feel more left out than not being dressed the way his friends are. Giving teenagers a clothing allowance and insisting they stay within it helps to make them more cautious about what they buy.

There is more to an acceptable personal appearance of course than the clothing that is worn. Teenagers often confuse "casual" with "sloppy" when really they are not the same. Girls spend a lot of time applying makeup base and false eyelashes but sometimes forget to wash behind the ears or the back of the neck. Girls don't need to be urged to fix their hair but they do need counsel on proper styling. Extremes are fun to fool around with and can be worn occasionally. The point is to watch where and when. This is another instance where even though everyone wears it, one style isn't automatically right for every individual.

DRIVING MANNERS

Teenage driving can be not only a courtesy problem but a safety problem as well. Driver education in school is helping to impress young people with the seriousness of knowing and obeying traffic laws. But parents have the ultimate responsibility of cracking down on disobedience by not allowing use of the car.

And of course parental example is as important here as in other matters.

GROUP BEHAVIOR IN PUBLIC

One teenage discourtesy that adults react against is loud talking and laughing in public places and on public transportation. Even though an individual has been brought up to be considerate of others, he can be easily swept up in the spirit of a group and be rude without realizing it. Often the noise is not harmful to anyone, but it is always discourteous to force others to be the unwilling overhearers of loud conversations.

What about a church group which sings gospel songs and choruses on a bus or train or in a restaurant without asking permission to do so? The argument that this is giving a testimony is open to question if those listening are so annoyed that they miss the gospel message. Of course the Holy Spirit is able to work in someone's heart and use the singing in spite of its annoyance to others.

But perhaps a group might consider what effect they would have on observers if they were well behaved and perhaps gave a quiet word of testimony to those sitting beside them. They should consider too how they would react if a group whose beliefs they did not share, forced them to listen to loud songs in public places. Someone might argue that a Christian group has as much right to sing in a restaurant as someone has to put money in the jukebox and force others to listen just because they are there. Actually neither is right. Loud talking and singing in public by anyone is an infringement of other people's rights and is not good manners.

Other teenage discourtesies often mentioned are monopolizing the telephone, not keeping rooms clean, staying out past deadlines, not being on time for meals. But all of these are the parents' responsibility to set wise limits and hold to them. They must know when to hold the line and when to make exceptions.

FAMILY STANDARDS VS FRIENDS' STANDARDS

Parents should try to let their children conform as much as possible to the standards of their friends and the customs of the community. But there are times when a parent feels his family has to go it alone regardless of what others do. If so, he must talk the situation over with his children and explain his convictions quietly, calmly and sincerely. If this has been done consistently through the years on other matters instead of simply forcing the child always to bow to the heavy hand of parental authority, there will be cooperation even though it may be reluctant.

Naturally parents cannot go everywhere with their children to be sure they are maintaining the standards set in the home. But the Christian parent can claim for his children the confidence expressed by Paul in Philippians 1:6 that "he which hath begun a good work in you will perform it until the day of Jesus Christ."

The basic rules given throughout these chapters apply to the teenager in all his behavior. Naturally he is more informal with his own group in the matter of making introductions and in conversation and in letter writing. When a bunch of teenagers get together for pizza they don't bother with a tablecloth and center-piece. But the basic rule of good manners—considering others before oneself—is theirs to conform to just as it is for any age.

For a Christian young person, the words of Paul in I Timothy 4:12 have particular meaning: "Let no man despise thy youth; but be thou an example of the believers, in word, in conversation, in charity, in spirit, in faith, in purity."

11

COLLEGE AND EMPLOYED SINGLE ADULTS

Paul reminds the Christians in one of his letters of how "holily and justly and unblameably we behaved ourselves among you" (I Thessalonians 2:10). This is a goal all of us should strive for. An aid to reaching it is found in the advice in Philippians 4:8: "Finally, brethren, whatsoever things are true, whatsoever things are honest, whatsoever things are just, whatsoever things are pure, whatsoever things are lovely, whatsoever things are of good report . . . think on these things."

IMPACT OF HOME TRAINING

College age usually marks the end of direct home supervision for a young person. This is as true of those who live at home and attend college or have a job as it is of those who go away to school or for employment. Legally a young person is not a voting adult until he is twenty-one, but he is expected to behave like one when he is through high school. Adults expect him to be mature in his responses and actions and attitudes. He in turn expects adults to know that he is able to make his own decisions and act independent of parental restrictions. Unfortunately, expectations are often too high on both sides of the fence.

The conventions and rules of childhood can't be thrown away as obsolete when one reaches a certain magic age. They are still important, and are followed because the person himself knows he should, not just because he is forced to do so by someone older. If there has been a good child-parent relationship through the years, there is not as much chance that the young person going away from home will turn from the manners and standards he has been taught.

It is always the responsibility of the home to prepare the children to stand up to whatever situations they meet. A college administration can't be expected either to teach manners and morals from scratch or to reinforce something that was never really learned in the first place.

GETTING ALONG WITH OTHERS

Correct behavior for living at college is the same as it is anywhere. Everybody wants to be liked, and the only way to be liked is to be likable. Good manners are absolutely essential for successful dormitory living. People can live together and be rude and inconsiderate, but it won't be successful living.

The person who learned to be polite and kind only to those he knows and likes, is in for a rude awakening at college. Two freshmen assigned to each other may be at opposite poles in tastes, habits, background and goals; but they have to somehow adapt to each other. This is easier to do if the main emphasis of true etiquette, considering others before oneself, was learned in childhood. Of course, sometimes this is one-sided, with one roommate showing good manners all year and the other not bothering. But college is a good place to practice the important quality of adaptability because all through life we are with people we don't like and don't agree with, and yet we have to get along with them peacefully. Sometimes in the process we find that we are not as easy to live with as we thought we were.

DORM MANNERS

Good manners for roommates mean not leaving the bathroom in a mess; cleaning the tub after using it; not making a lot of noise or keeping the light burning and the radio blasting late at night (nor on the other hand going to bed too early and demanding total silence); not borrowing constantly; not taking more than one's share of closet or drawer space; not using someone else's toothpaste, shampoo or soap; hanging up clothes and putting away personal belongings; and keeping one's share of the room clean.

Proper etiquette for college students means politeness to other students and respect for their views even though they are completely different. It means being polite to faculty members, to staff, to those who wait on them in the dining room or bookstore. It means making proper introductions and practicing acceptable table manners and being personally clean and all the other ordinary, commonsense politeness that makes living in a group pleasanter.

Why all this? Bluntly, so people will like you. Friends are always better than enemies. Why else? So that the testimony the Christian student takes with him to college is easier for the nonchristian student to accept because it is a part of a likable person.

COLLEGE RULES

Most colleges have rules—about hours, clothes, employment, paying bills, cars, social activities—and these should be observed. The student who actively disagrees with college rules and cannot reconcile himself to them should leave and go to a school where the regulations are more to his liking. He doesn't have the right either to flout them or try to change them by rebelling against them outside of legitimate channels or by inciting others to rebel. There are too many demanding a college education to allow a campus to be crowded by those who are only interested in agitating, not in learning.

DEVELOPING BAD HABITS

One of the aspects of college life that parents fear is that their children will take up practices and develop habits they have not previously had. Using drugs, drinking, smoking, excessive petting, premarital sex, rebellion against rules of any kind on college campuses, make headlines in the newspapers. We lament the lessening of the moral fiber of young people who find a conflict between childhood training and the opinions of those with different training.

MORAL ISSUES

But it is the college person himself who must stand for what he believes. No one can force him to say or do or think anything he does not want to. The general philosophy in many places is to be reasonable in one's attitude toward drinking and smoking and premarital sex and to follow a course of moderation. This is like playing with a little bit of fire; it can get out of hand easily and cause fatal burns.

What do these moral issues have to do with college etiquette? Simply that good manners come from the heart. What is inside a man determines the kind of person he is. He may be outwardly correct and fastidious, but if there is rottenness within it will come to the surface.

The young person on a college campus because of his advantage of a higher education is potentially a leader. A leader must be morally upright. The Christian on the college campus has a Helper, the Holy Spirit, who gives the courage and the ability to remain "unspotted from the world" (James 1:27).

SINGLE ADULT AT HOME

The single adult, whether he went to college or not, has a code of good manners to observe also. If he lives at home, he is in a sense independent of parental rules about the hours he keeps, how he spends his money, where and when he goes on vacation, the friends he has, how he dresses. Yet this very freedom is binding because it puts on him the added burden of responsibility for his own conduct.

He cannot be independent of others in the house. Whether or not he pays board and room is immaterial, for he himself must still regulate his behavior. He may come in at 3:00 A.M. instead of by an 11:00 P.M. parental deadline, but he still has to be quiet. He cannot run the shower full blast or turn the stereo on loud or bring his friends in for a party at that hour because then he infringes on the rights of others. If he invites friends in for meals or for a weekend, he must still clear it with the one responsible for running the household. If he uses the family car, he must ask permission to do so and expect to pay for gas and oil.

In short, as long as he is under the family roof, he must live in a way that other people can live comfortably with him.

Often single young adults think all their problems of independence will be solved by moving into their own apartment or away from a small town or suburb into a big city. The move may achieve this goal, but it may also open new problems.

BACHELOR LIVING ALONE

Young men have always had more freedom in their social life than single girls. This remains true when they move from home into their own apartment or one shared with another bachelor. But a young man must still observe the rules of good manners in his appearance, his behavior with others, his conversation, his social life and his business contacts. It is not out of line to include in proper etiquette for young men the command of Scripture to "flee also youthful lusts: but follow righteousness, faith, charity, peace" (II Timothy 2:22).

SINGLE GIRL IN HER APARTMENT

The many single girls who set up their own apartments in a big city away from home often find that life is not as glamorous as they had expected. Even if they are able to manage the expenses of an apartment alone, it is a lonely life. The girl living alone often does not bother to prepare nourishing meals. She may let the cleaning slide since there is no one to see the dirt but herself. The single girl alone has a problem when she wants to entertain. Inviting friends in for a meal sometimes wrecks the week's food budget and always means extra work which she must do alone. Entertaining a man friend for a meal or for the evening can be a problem also. While society does not frown on this as it once did, there is still a certain amount of risk involved, particularly if he is a casual acquaintance whom she does not know well. There is a lack of protection even in a large apartment building, as stories in the newspapers repeatedly make clear.

SHARING AN APARTMENT

If a girl can find one or more congenial roommates with whom to live, it helps to cut expenses and provides companionship and protection. Etiquette for roommates in these circumstances is the same as it is any time people live together. It won't always be smooth sailing. In fact, a girl should be careful with whom she signs a year's lease, lest it turn out to be twelve months of constant friction. All roommates have to learn to yield a little on nonessentials.

There must be agreement about how to share the

expenses. The rent must be divided evenly, the groceries bought jointly, the basic phone bill divided equally with each one paying her own toll calls and long-distance bills. Cooking, cleaning and laundering chores have to be shared equally either by all pitching in to do a little of each job or one doing the cooking, another the cleaning, and so on.

Single girls in a shared apartment have more opportunity for a social life with men because they can invite them in for a meal or for the evening with the understanding that there is a roommate somewhere in the background. This is an area where single young adults must be careful to "abstain from all appearance of evil" (I Thessalonians 5:22).

In I Thessalonians 1:7-8 Paul told the Christians that they were such good examples and gave such clear evidence of what they believed, that their "faith to Godward is spread abroad; so that we need not to speak anything." The young person striking out on his own is only doing what his parents have been preparing him to do. The way he behaves will show whether he has been given a heritage of good manners.

12

BUSINESS COURTESY

Ephesians 5:19—6:9 outlines the various relationships of life and makes clear that it is the way we live in them which proves whether we are filled with the Holy Spirit. One of these is the employer-employee relationship in Ephesians 6:5-9. Each person is to act toward another as though he were actually serving God. Earning a living often becomes just a dreary routine, a dog-eat-dog existence, when it should be done in a gracious "with good will doing service, as to the Lord" spirit.

PRACTICAL VALUE

The man or woman who is a gracious host or hostess or an appreciative guest may turn into an overbearing tyrant in the business world because he does not realize that etiquette—practicing good manners—can help him run a business smoothly. The same manners should be used in business as in social life. After all, it is just sound business sense to be courteous and gracious and so make friends instead of enemies.

Courtesy to fellow employees, respect to those in authority, and a sincere desire to do one's best should be the attitude of everyone in the business world and especially of the Christian.

MANNERS FOR THE EMPLOYER

For the employer this business etiquette includes honesty in his dealings with others, fair treatment of those who work for him, a courteous attitude toward each one, and consideration of the rights of each. But it also includes expecting that each one will do his job to capacity. The employer who allows those in his charge to be slothful has only himself to blame for a poorly run business.

MANNERS FOR THE EMPLOYEE

One of the most important qualifications an employee can develop is faithfulness. A worker certainly has a right to complain if he does not receive a full paycheck at the end of the month; but an employer also has a right to complain if his workers do not give full value in the work they do during the month. This includes putting in a full day's work by arriving on time and working until quitting time. Few employers object to a secretary writing personal letters if she is caught up on her work, but they do object to her doing so when the IN basket is overflowing. Standard procedure in an office or business of any kind should include working instead of chatting with fellow workers, not overstaying a coffee break or lunch hour, not wasting office supplies.

This behavior is right for the Christian whether employed in a Christian or a secular firm. In Colossians 3:22-23 God in speaking to servants (employees in our terminology) says, "And whatsoever ye do, do it heartily, as to the Lord, and not unto men."

Efficiency should be the first consideration in a

business office or store, and everyone from the boss to the janitor or cleaning woman should contribute to this goal by doing his work conscientiously.

BUSINESS RELATIONSHIPS

This doesn't mean that the atmosphere in a business establishment, large or small, must be formal and cold in order to be efficient. We are quite casual today in our social relationships, and this carries over into the business world as well. Of course some people think that to be friendly everyone must be on a first-name basis. And so Miss, Mrs. and Mr. are thrown out in favor of Mary, Sally and Joe. This is all right if the employer feels that it results in greater efficiency in the business and in greater harmony among the staff. The use of first names is common in a small business where the office staff works more closely together than it does in a large firm.

But there can be some danger here because of the various levels of authority and responsibility that have to be a part of the business world. There is an unofficial caste system in most large business offices whereby those in higher positions can be friendly toward everyone, but those in lower positions are considered climbers if they are overly friendly.

Sometimes first-naming can be interpreted as patronizing rather than friendly, or impudent rather than genuinely warm. It is understandable if the president of the company calls the elevator boy "Tom," but for Tom to respond with "Good morning, Harry" isn't good manners. On the other hand, if the elevator operator is an elderly man, he may want—and deserve

—the respect of Mr. even from the company president. There is a middle road in the business of first names which may be safer in the long run. In this, a degree of formality is maintained during business hours, along with friendliness, and the first names are reserved for after business hours. People who are in equal positions in business call each other by the name they would use socially. Certainly even if everyone is on a first-name basis within the office, titles are used when speaking to or about each other in the presence of those who are not part of the office family. This degree of formality helps to forestall close confidences that may be made too hastily and regretted later.

The one in the office who seems on the surface to be the most friendly may not be genuinely so. This is particularly true in the cutthroat competition of a modern office where one man will trample on others if it is to his personal advantage. The one who does this may get ahead, but at the cost of the goodwill of others. The worker in a Christian organization should be aware that such things can happen there also, for each of us is human and the ego is quick to seek personal advancement. The man who is seeking his own good rather than that of the establishment is often obsequious to those above him, inconsiderate of his equals and contemptuous of those beneath him. The Scripture speaks on this point when it says, "Let no man seek his own, but every man another's wealth [welfare]" (I Corinthians 10:24).

It seems to be true that the more important a person is, the more courteous he is. Top men are often more considerate of others and more approachable than those on the way up. This may be one reason they are in positions of leadership.

PERSONAL LIFE IN BUSINESS

One's personal life should not be allowed to intrude into working hours. Personal messages over the phone are sometimes unavoidable, but friends should be discouraged from phoning the office just to chat. And of course personal calls to arrange one's social life should be kept to a minimum.

THE WORKING MOTHER

A working mother finds this a more acute problem than a woman without children, because she cannot simply forget her children while she is working. It's best for the working mother to have an understanding with her employer that there may be times she will have to stay home because of a family emergency. She must try to be as efficient as possible while she is on the job to make up for those other times.

WOMEN IN BUSINESS

A woman who is employed away from home must learn to be quick and accurate and impersonal, whether she is a top executive or just a file clerk; at the same time she must keep her femininity. She should use her charm not to get ahead but to keep things running smoothly in her particular part of the work.

The woman in business has particular disadvantages to overcome. The chief of these is the difficulty of learning to be impersonal in business dealings. All of her natural personal feelings, prejudices, likes and dislikes must be subordinated for the good of the work. This is true for women in responsible positions who are in charge of others, as well as for secretaries and typists.

SECRETARY'S RELATIONSHIP TO EMPLOYER

A secretary should not expect that her boss will rise when she enters his office the way he would for a woman visitor or the way he would for her if they met socially. Nor should she expect him to overlook carelessness on her part just because she is a woman. The secretary must give wholehearted loyalty to her employer by not only refraining from talking about him, but not listening if others do. She must keep his business confidences and show her respect for him to other employees. If she cannot do so honestly, she should not be in that position of trust.

An employer must remember that "please" and "thank you" have a place in the business world and accomplish more than a curt order. When it is necessary to correct a worker for mistakes, it should be done quietly and not in the presence of others.

PERSONAL APPEARANCE, DRESS

One's personal appearance in the business world reflects not only personal qualities but those of the business as well. (See chapter on Personal Behavior.) The office atmosphere often influences the type of clothing that is worn. For example, a large law office in a big city which handles accounts for huge corporations may expect its employees to dress more formally than a surburban real estate office which hires housewives on a part-time basis as the office staff.

Women especially must subordinate their personal taste in clothing if they are employed in the business world. Low necklines, tight sweaters, extremely short or tight skirts or dresses, and bracelets that jangle with every movement are out of place in a business. A sweater and skirt are really too casual for an older woman even though a young girl may wear them. One is always right wearing a tailored dress or suit, though it should not be too severe, or a dressy blouse and well-fitted skirt. Extremes in clothes, hairstyles or jewelry are definitely out in the business world. Heavy eye makeup is better kept for evening wear. Most women keep an extra supply of cosmetics in a desk drawer for touching up during the day. This is a good idea, but any repairing of makeup should be done in the washroom rather than at the desk.

To say that a woman in business should be well-groomed means that she is clean, neat, with well-pressed clothes, conservative in dress rather than either casual or extreme, and wearing a minimum of jewelry and makeup.

Men find it less possible to go astray in the matter of clothing because there is less variety in what they wear. (See chapter on Personal Behavior for further discussion of men's clothing.)

Men and women both need to remember that sometimes deodorant and mouth wash ads are laughed off when they should be taken personally.

TELEPHONE COURTESY

Telephone manners in an office are somewhat different from those used at home. Courtesy is still the primary consideration and this is best shown by the voice. Those calling receive an impression of an entire business establishment from the voice of the one who answers the telephone. An impatient or indifferent tone is noticed and remembered by the caller. Carelessness on the part of the switchboard operator in putting through a call may lose business and goodwill for the company.

An executive should answer his own phone if it rings right at his elbow and he is not busy. It isn't necessary for every call to go through the secretary. But when he is busy and the secretary does answer, remembering that efficiency is her goal and that company time is valuable, she does not say, "Hello." The proper greeting from an office is "Good morning, Mr. Employer's office" or "Mr. Employer's office, Miss Blank speaking" or "Good afternoon, XYZ Company."

Then when the caller asks for Mr. Employer, the secretary says, "Just a moment, please" and transfers the call. If she knows her boss is not in the office or that he is in conference, she tells the caller so and asks, "May I help you?" or says, "If you will leave your name, I'll tell him you called." If the name is left or a message given, be sure to write it down rather than trusting your memory to recall it several hours later.

The point is to identify the business and make it clear that the one answering the phone is in a position to help. Friendliness and courtesy are expressed by the tone of voice as well as by the words that are spoken. The "Good morning, Mr. Employer's office" can be curt and cold or warm and helpful, depending on the way in which the words are said.

When someone places a call to a company which has several departments, he should first ask the switchboard operator for the department he wants and then, when he is connected, ask for the person: "May I speak to Mr. Jones, please? This is John Smith of XYZ Company." When there are no departments, the caller gives his name and company identification directly to the switchboard operator.

When a call comes in, it isn't always wise for the secretary to ask who is calling and then say that the employer isn't available. The caller may suspect that he really is—to those he wants to talk to. The secretary must handle each situation as tactfully as possible both for the caller and for her boss. Protecting him is her first responsibility, and yet she must do so without losing contacts or business for him.

WHAT ABOUT THE BUSINESS LIE?

Sometimes an executive does not wish to talk to a caller, either by phone or in person, but it is not good business for the secretary to say so. This is one place where a secretary runs into what has politely been called the business lie—saying the boss is in conference when actually he is not. There are many other similar occasions in the business world in which lying is standard procedure. Most employers will respect the scruples of an employee if he explains his convictions in these matters, and will try to work out a satisfactory system of handling such problems. Obeying the command to "give none offence" can be difficult. But it has been proven that the Lord honors the Christian who maintains a standard pleasing to Him in the business world as well as in private life.

All that is said about appearance and cleanliness and courteous behavior applies to those who clerk in stores or are waiters and waitresses or meet the public in any capacity. They have the added burden of having close contact with customers who are not always as polite as they should be. It is inexcusable for anyone to think someone else is inferior just because he waits on others.

APPLYING FOR A JOB IN PERSON

What was said earlier in the chapter about dress is particularly important for those seeking a job. Appearance speaks either for or against the person who is being interviewed. Clothing, voice, hairstyle or the words one uses may offset the natural aptitude one may have for a job. These points must be checked carefully, especially by the one being interviewed for a first job when he has no experience to offer.

You should be on time for an interview and be prepared to answer questions about your goals in life and the type of work you are best qualified to do. Be self-confident but not cocky. Don't attempt either to build yourself up unduly or run down the last employer and those you worked with. Also don't be too eager to ask about the salary and all the fringe benefits that come with the job. If you are asked what salary you expect, be ready to name a realistic figure. Don't chew gum or interrupt with questions of your own.

The interviewer should take the lead in asking questions, but should give the applicant opportunity to ask some also. He should put the applicant at ease and not be too stern. It is he who indicates when the interview is over, and the applicant should leave promptly.

WRITTEN JOB APPLICATION

In writing an application for a job, list name, address, telephone number, age, whether married, draft status (for men), education and experience. Be sure this is legible even if it means you must print. Beginning with the most recent, list previous jobs in the order they were held and include the dates of employment, the name of the business, description of the work done, salary received and the reason for leaving. Be completely honest about this, for incorrect information has a way of catching up with a person. For a first job with no previous experience (and for others when asked), give several references of people who are not relatives.

Everyone in business should remember that the boorish, ill-mannered man does not get the promotions. Some may object that it is insincere to pretend to manners just for the practical advantages that might follow. But even if the manners are not genuine, it is better to put them on than not to show them at all; they may through use become second nature. This is not being deceitful. Many times in life we have to smile and be polite when we would rather scowl and be rude. This is where the admonition of Scripture comes with force to the Christian in the business world: "Let your conversation [behavior] be as it becometh the gospel of Christ" (Philippians 1:27).

13

PUBLIC SPEAKING AND PARLIAMENTARY ETIQUETTE

Some people can make a speech or give a report or conduct a meeting with no fear and perfectly at ease. To others, speaking in public is a harrowing experience. Knowing the fundamental rules of speaking and conducting meetings helps to make the experience less frightening. This is another place where the Christian can learn to "walk worthy of the Lord unto all pleasing" (Colossians 1:10).

CHARACTERISTICS OF A SPEAKER

Most of us at some time stand to speak before a group, if only at a PTA, church or club meeting. The person who is brief, speaks clearly, can be heard, and has something of worth to say, is appreciated by an audience. Though few people are born with this talent, everyone can learn to improve his speaking ability. All that has been said previously about good manners comes into play when one speaks in public. A pleasing personal appearance, a tactful manner and an attitude of respect for people must be characteristics of the one who speaks to convince others.

SPEAKING LOUDLY ENOUGH, CLEARLY

An audience reacts favorably to a pleasant, well-modulated, expressive voice. A woman particularly must learn correct voice placement so that she pitches her voice low enough not to be shrill and yet loud enough to be heard clearly. No matter how good the message, if the speaker can't be heard, it does no good. Often a microphone will be available, but for the many times when it will not be, each one should train his voice so that it can be heard. This is possible by practicing good posture, correct breathing, being sufficiently relaxed, and really caring about improving speaking ability. When standing among a group to speak, one should try to address the person farthest away.

Many people talk too fast so that it's difficult for those listening to catch the sense of the words. About a hundred words a minute, or a half page of typed material, is a fast enough rate when speaking to a group. This will not seem too slow if the voice is animated and expressive.

USING GOOD GRAMMAR

In speaking to a group of any size it is important to use correct grammar and to pronounce words accurately. Incorrect grammar in private conversation may be excused as just a slip of the tongue. But such mistakes are much more obvious in a public speech and may cause the speaker to lose the respect of the audience. One very critical lady in a church was willing to listen to the gospel message because the new minister correctly used words which she considered important. This is something every speaker can learn because it is simply a matter of using the dictionary.

USING UNDERSTANDABLE WORDS

The words of a speech must be immediately understood. A written message can be reread to pick up obscure points, but a spoken message can't be. While a certain amount of repetition of ideas is possible, and even necessary in a speech, those who listen must understand the meaning of the words the first time they hear them. Use short, concrete, familiar words in brief sentences. This does not insult the intelligence of those in the audience, but shows consideration for them. The one who uses big words, involved sentences and technical language is like the one who speaks in an unknown tongue, "for no man understandeth him" (I Corinthians 14:2).

PRACTICING A SPEECH

Most of us need to spend time preparing a speech. There are some who can speak extemporaneously with facts and material organized, the right words at the tip of the tongue, and have good rapport with the audience almost effortlessly. This is not true of most speakers. Often an apparently extemporaneous speech is the result of long hours of practice and polish. One should not read a speech if at all possible, but it is better to do so than to try to speak extemporaneously and wander aimlessly in a wilderness of words without meaning. It's possible to practice reading a speech so that it can be done without being too obvious.

SPEAKER'S MANNER

The manner of the one speaking is important whether he is giving a rehearsed speech, rising in a discussion to contribute a point, or conducting a meeting. He should be able to speak with assurance and knowledge and conviction. But along with this he must be courteous. This is especially true for the Christian minister preaching a sermon or a layman giving a testimony. We are not to argue, to ridicule, to lambaste others. The words in Colossians 4:6 fit here: "Let your speech be always with grace, seasoned with salt, that ye may know how ye ought to answer every man." (See chapter on Conversation.)

PERSONAL APPEARANCE

All that has been said about personal appearance is important for the one who stands before others to speak. A funny hat on a woman, too much makeup, a too tight or too short skirt, or wrinkled stockings will take attention from her words. An ill-fitting suit or the light reflecting from a man's tie clip will have the same effect. In addition any nervous habit such as constantly shifting one's glasses or tapping a pencil on a table or using too many gestures can distract an audience. The speaker's posture when sitting on the platform or standing to speak affects audience response. Women must be particularly careful when sitting in front of a group. Crossing one leg over another is the least flattering way for a woman to sit.

No matter how inadequate you feel as a speaker, don't tell your audience. It creates a negative impression which you will have to work to overcome. Don't apologize for your lack of preparation and knowledge or protest your lack of qualifications to speak. This usually sounds like false modesty. If it's true, it will soon be apparent to those listening; if not, you only sound insincere.

Perhaps you feel you will never be asked to speak before a group, and if you were, you would refuse because this is not your gift. There is still one type of meeting in which you will undoubtedly take part at some time. This is the business meeting. Everyone should be familiar with the rules that govern it so that he knows what to do as a member of the group or as the chairman. Whether it is a small group or a large one, a women's missionary organization or a legislature, the same basic rules are used in conducting the business.

CONDUCTING A BUSINESS MEETING

So many meetings are poorly conducted and much time wasted simply because the one presiding and those sitting in the group do not know how to carry on the business efficiently. There is really no excuse for this because the basic parliamentary rules are quite simple and can be easily learned. One should know the rules and then use them properly.

PARLIAMENTARY PROCEDURE

Of course parliamentary procedure as it is carried on in lawmaking bodies is much more complicated than that of the average church board or women's club meeting. But the main purpose remains the same—to conduct business in an orderly way, to find the majority will, and to protect the rights of the minority group. Anyone can learn to conduct a meeting properly and participate in the discussions intelligently.

Robert's *Rules of Order* can be checked out of any library and will give a great deal of detail about parliamentary rules, more than most of us will ever use.

Conducting a business meeting correctly comes under the classification of good manners. Knowing what to do and how to do it keeps the one presiding from becoming flustered and helps him maintain poise to keep others in the meeting from showing bad manners.

A QUORUM

A quorum must be present to officially conduct business. This simply means enough of the membership to legally vote on measures and pass resolutions. Sometimes a two-thirds majority is required to pass a motion and sometimes a simple majority is enough. Every member has equal rights and privileges in stating his views, but the majority vote always carries a resolution.

SECRETARY'S REPORT

A business meeting is opened by the chairman who says, "Will the meeting please come to order?" and then asks the secretary to read the minutes of the last meeting. These should include the name of the group, the date, place and hour of the meeting, whether the minutes of the previous meeting were approved, any motions made and seconded and by whom, what action was taken on them, and the time of adjournment. If this is a women's missionary meeting, it isn't necessary that the secretary include in the minutes a detailed review of the message. The minutes are signed

"Respectfully submitted" (*not* respectively) with the secretary's name. The chairman then asks, "Are there any additions or corrections to the minutes?" He waits a moment and if there are none, he says, "The minutes stand approved as read," or, if there were corrections, "as corrected." The secretary notes the approval either at the beginning or end of the minutes. If a copy of the minutes was sent to each member ahead of time, it is not necessary to read them at the meeting. The chairman asks if there are corrections to the minutes as received before declaring them acceptable.

TREASURER'S REPORT

If there is a treasurer's report it is given, but group approval is not always asked since the members have no way of knowing on the spot if the money was handled correctly. The chairman says, "The treasurer's report is received and will be filed for audit."

If there are committee chairmen, each is called on for a report even though there may not necessarily be a report at each meeting. Then old or unfinished business is cared for, followed by new business.

CONTROLLED DISCUSSION

One of the most difficult jobs of the presiding officer is to control discussion and not to allow one member to dominate and keep others from expressing an opinion. He must be polite and tactful, and yet able to step in with a firm "Thank you for your comments, Mr. Blank. Is there additional discussion?" The chairman must also keep the discussion to the subject and not allow members to wander off into side issues.

MAKING A MOTION

Sometimes there is misunderstanding about when discussion takes place in a business meeting. There must be a proposition before the group in order to have a discussion. For example, a motion is made as follows: "I move [or make a motion] that we take twenty-five dollars from the treasury to send to the New Life project." If no one seconds the motion, the chairman asks, "Is there a second?" If there is none, the matter is dropped. If someone seconds it (and this must be recorded by the secretary), the chairman restates the motion: "It has been moved and seconded that . . ." and then asks if there is any discussion. Note that if there is no motion, there is nothing to discuss. All motions should be stated affirmatively so that a yes vote means action is taken, and a no vote refuses action. A motion may be amended during the discussion.

TAKING THE VOTE

After the discussion the chairman asks, "Are you ready for the question?" Sometimes a member calls for the question, particularly when the discussion seems to be going on indefinitely and members are only repeating themselves. Then before calling for the vote, which may be by voice, by standing, by a show of hands, by roll call or by secret ballot, the chairman repeats the motion or asks the secretary to read it.

The chairman does *not* say, "Those in favor signify by the usual sign." The proper expression is "Those in favor of the motion say 'Aye'; those opposed, 'No.' "

After the vote he says either "The motion is carried" or "The motion is not carried."

Only one item of business can be considered at a time and no new business can be brought up until the first is settled.

ADJOURNING THE MEETING

The only motion that does not require discussion is a motion to adjourn a meeting. When this is made, seconded and carried, the chairman states, "The meeting is adjourned" even if there should be protests from the minority. Or if all the business has been finished the chairman may say, "Is there anything more to come before the meeting?" If no one responds, the chairman can declare the meeting adjourned.

Many meetings are held informally in a home, or after an evening church service, or just before another meeting, and it may seem unnecessary to follow even these simple rules. Yet important business has often been carried on in very small, informal situations. It's a good idea to have minutes kept even of the briefest meetings to know what motions were made and what action was taken, and to preserve through this formality a sense of responsibility in business. As in all rules of etiquette, there is safety in knowing what should be done even though it may not always have to be done to the last detail.

The Apostle Paul wanted Timothy to be aware of certain things so that he would know "how to behave himself in the household of faith." Doing things "decently and in order" (I Corinthians 14:40) is good sense always as well as good manners.

14

TRAVEL ETIQUETTE

The fact that we are "compassed about with so great a cloud of witnesses" is a reason the writer to the Hebrews gives for living a consistent Christian life (Hebrews 12:1). This can be applied to those who travel away from home. There is never an excuse for bad manners no matter where we are, though those who know us may overlook them. Those who don't, can't excuse bad manners or rude behavior. Knowing how to behave while traveling helps us give a "good profession before manv witnesses" (I Timothy 6:12).

COMMUTING COURTESIES

Whether the traveling we do is just the commuting to work each day or a vacation trip to Hawaii or around the world, good manners are essential. They are the same ones we should always observe, but sometimes we forget them when we go away from home.

Much of our commuting is done by bus, subway, elevated or train, and no one can live to himself on public transportation. Basic good manners require having the fare ready in advance, not pushing past others to get a seat, moving to the rear of the bus when necessary, getting off at the proper door, not reading a newspaper so that it bothers others, not smoking or talking loudly or annoying others in any way, not letting a young child occupy a seat alone if others who have paid a fare are standing. All these are simple rules of courtesy which we would like others to practice toward us.

TAXI MANNERS

When taking a taxi one should expect to tip the driver. In smaller towns tipping may not be expected, but in most communities it is, and the driver's salary may be based on the fact that he will receive tips. In a cab with a meter, you pay the fare that is registered when you reach your destination plus the tip, which is usually 15 percent of the bill. In some towns a flat rate is set depending on the distance you are going. Often an extra charge is made for handling baggage. If two or more passengers going to different places ride at the same time, each one pays what is registered on the meter when he gets out, plus his tip.

It isn't necessary to strike up a conversation with the driver or with other passengers, but interest in others is a large part of courtesy. If one is really concerned about witnessing, genuine, warm friendliness will be honored by the Lord, whatever the circumstances.

In rush hours when cabs are hard to get, it is usually on a first-come-first-get basis even in the case of men and women. It would be very gracious of a man to allow a woman to have a cab he has just managed to hail, but it is by no means obligatory. Just because she is a woman does not mean she has more right to the taxi than he. She may only be going to a party while he may be rushing to catch a plane.

DRIVING ETIQUETTE

A great deal of traveling is done by car. It seems to be a peculiarity of the human race that a person who is courteous in most other situations loses respect for others when he gets behind the wheel of a car. Safety statistics show that a large part of the death and accident rate is due to impoliteness of drivers. Drinking, failure to yield the right of way, running stop signs, not signaling properly, not giving pedestrians their rights, are poor driving manners which result in accidents. Driving etiquette becomes a life and death matter.

Manners for the driver include obeying all rules of the road, dimming bright lights for oncoming traffic, being considerate of pedestrians, keeping children protected, not becoming too absorbed in conversation. Passengers have equal responsibility not to annoy the driver and to keep children quiet and occupied. No one should ever throw anything out a car window.

By all means wear comfortable clothes when traveling by car. But if you expect to stop in restaurants for meals, plan your clothes with this in mind. It's true that many people do go into restaurants in any old thing—but you know how they look.

MOTEL AND HOTEL RESERVATIONS

To insure a motel room it is wise to make a reservation rather than to count on finding a vacancy when you arrive. If you stop early enough in the day, there are often vacancies but perhaps not at the larger, better motels.

To reserve a room in a hotel it is usually best to write or wire ahead and specify exactly what is wanted. For example:

> Please reserve a room with bath for my wife and me for October 9-16. We prefer not to be higher than the fifth floor.
>
>   Yours truly,
>
>   *John Smith*

If you ask for a confirmation of the reservation, be sure to give your address.

REGISTERING IN A HOTEL

When you arrive at the hotel, the bellhop takes the luggage and waits by the desk while you register. A man signs the register "John Smith, San Francisco" or, if his family is with him, "Mr. and Mrs. John Smith and children" if they are small. Older children sign the register themselves. If a woman is traveling alone, she signs "Miss Mary Smith" or "Mrs. John Smith," one of the few times a woman uses "Mrs." in her handwritten signature.

When you have registered, the clerk gives the bellhop the key and you follow him to the elevator. He unlocks the door of the room, goes in ahead of you, turns on the lights and the air conditioner or opens the windows (in warm weather), and waits for his tip.

TIPPING IN A HOTEL

Anyone who travels must expect to tip. The quality

of the hotel, the amount and kind of luggage you have, the service you expect, and your appearance determine the amount you tip those who do things for you. A woman wearing a mink coat is expected to tip more generously than one wearing a cloth coat, whether this seems fair or not.

A waiter in a hotel dining room receives the usual 15 percent of the bill. There is increasing pressure for this to rise to 20 percent but you can justly and firmly resist this. Never leave less than twenty-five cents if you sit at a table with a cloth no matter how little you order. The headwaiter is tipped in proportion to the service he gives; if he does nothing for you, you needn't tip him. Room waiters are given 10 to 15 percent of the bill; bellhops twenty-five cents a bag. A doorman who gets a cab for you is tipped a minimum of twenty-five cents. If he has parked the car and gets it for you, he is tipped fifty cents.

MEALS IN A HOTEL

Hotels vary in their arrangements for meals and room. In the American plan the cost of the meals is included in the price of the room. In the European plan, which is used by most hotels in our country, the meals are extra. You may have your meals in your room if you prefer, but remember that a service charge will be added to the stated price of the meal. This is not the waiter's tip; he is tipped in addition to the service charge.

Any reputable hotel frowns on out-of-line behavior and may ask guests to leave if there are doubts about them. One should behave in a hotel as one would as a guest in someone's home out of consideration for others who are staying there.

CHECKING OUT

When checking out of a hotel, you phone down to the desk and ask to have your bill ready and a bellhop sent to help with the luggage. You leave the key at the desk when you pay the bill. There is always a checking out time in a hotel and if you stay overtime, you have to pay for an extra day even though you don't stay over the night. You may always check out before the stated time, and then sit in the lobby if it is not time to leave for your train or plane. Sitting in the lobby is free and no one will look askance at you for doing so.

MOTEL ADVANTAGES

There are advantages to staying in a motel if you are traveling by car. There is no parking problem, no bellboy to tip; your car is immediately accessible just outside the door, and you need not see anyone after checking in at the office. You leave the key in the room when you go.

RESORT MANNERS

If you stay at a resort, you follow whatever rules are posted and observe the same basic principles of good manners you would anywhere else. You must be careful to observe dining room formalities regarding the wearing of bathing suits and other sport clothes.

BUS TRAVEL

On longer trips by bus or train, you must observe

certain rules of the road for your own comfort and that of fellow travelers. A cross-country trip on a bus is not the ordeal it once was. Many buses are air-conditioned, have reclining seats and rest rooms. But one is closer to fellow passengers, which means that loud conversations, crying children and noisy eating can be particularly annoying to others. The driver has a schedule to keep so that a rest or lunch stop is not the time to eat a leisurely meal. When lights are dimmed for sleeping on overnight trips, don't insist on your right to read late.

TRAIN TRAVEL

There is somewhat more room and privacy on a train, but one is still living in close quarters with others whether it is for a few hours or for two or three days. A coach seat is the least expensive way to travel by train. Some coaches have reserved seats for which you pay a little extra and you do not have to stand in line to be sure of getting one. When traveling by coach, wear comfortable clothes that do not wrinkle easily. Whether you bring a box meal to eat in your seat or buy sandwiches and beverages from the steward going through the coach, it's important to eat quietly and unobtrusively. Leftover food and wrappings must be disposed of so others do not have to see and smell them.

EATING IN DINING CAR

If you eat in the dining car, you may go as soon as the steward comes through the train announcing that meals are being served, or you may wait until later.

You act just as you would in any restaurant except that the order is written on paper supplied by the waiter rather than given verbally to him.

UPPER, LOWER BERTHS

When you buy a first-class ticket you travel pullman but you pay extra for your accommodations. The upper berth of course is cheaper. The one who has the lower berth is entitled during the day to the seat facing forward. You specify which you want when you make the reservation. The porter will ask when you want the berths made up, and since he will naturally want to have this done by ten or ten-thirty because of his many responsibilities, you should cooperate with him. While he is doing so, you may sit in any other empty seat in the car or in the lounge or club car since your ticket entitles you to this privilege.

You will probably dress and undress in your berth because there isn't much privacy or space in the washroom. The upper berth occupant would do well to use the washroom before undressing since the porter must bring a ladder to use in climbing in and out of the berth. If you have to get up during the night, you must ring for the porter to bring the ladder.

ROOMETTES, COMPARTMENTS

In addition to coach and pullman accommodations, one may also buy a roomette or a compartment; these have washbowl and toilet facilities. Reservations must be made and there is a charge in addition to the price of the ticket.

TIPPING ON TRAINS

Tipping is a necessary part of train travel. A porter receives twenty-five to fifty cents for assistance he gives during daytime travel, fifty cents to one dollar for an overnight trip by pullman, and more for service in a compartment or bedroom. The conductor is not tipped. The dining car steward is tipped just as in a restaurant. Those who handle suitcases in the baggage room are not tipped, but porters and redcaps in the station are usually given a fixed charge of twenty-five cents a bag and more for extra service. The redcap who gets a wheelchair for an elderly person and takes him to the right train should be tipped accordingly. If you want to carry your own bag, just say, "No, thank you" to the redcap who wants to take it. Most stations have carts for bags which passengers can use and the need for a redcap is eliminated.

FELLOW PASSENGERS

One doesn't want to look with suspicion on all one's fellow passengers and freeze at every friendly smile. Yet girls and women who travel alone do have to be cautious on buses and trains and not be too responsive to a seatmate, whether man or woman, who begins a conversation and asks personal questions. No one should give his name or address or other important information to a stranger. A girl should not allow a stranger to pay for her meals. If a man is persistent in talking and her polite disinterest does not discourage him, she should certainly ask for help from the conductor who is used to handling such matters.

PLANE RESERVATIONS

Reservations are essential for a plane trip regardless
of the length. You usually reserve the space rather
than a seat so that when you get on the plane you
generally may sit in any seat. On reaching your destination, be sure to confirm your return flight. If you
find it necessary to cancel a reservation, do it immediately so that the space may be sold to someone else.

Most jets have first-class, coach and economy
flights. Meals are included in the price of the first-class
or coach ticket. There is more room in the first-class
section since there are only two seats on each side of
the aisle. The meals in coach flights are not as elaborate as those in the first class. Economy flights do not
serve meals. The coach and economy flights may have
three seats on each side of the aisle or three on one
side and two on the other.

LUGGAGE LIMIT

One should be at the airport from a half hour to an
hour ahead of flight time to check in luggage and get
to the right gate on time. When you make your reservation find out how much baggage you are allowed.
There is no longer a weight restriction for travel within the United States, but there are regulations concerning the size of the luggage, both that which is checked
and any you carry with you. There is still a weight
limit for travel outside the United States.

On international flights it is forty-four pounds in
the tourist class and sixty-six pounds on the first-class
ticket. Even hand luggage aside from a purse is
counted in the total weight allotment. If extra baggage

is allowed (and it isn't always), the cost per pound is high. The luggage is weighed when you arrive at the airport and check in, and you must show the ticket stubs you receive when you claim your luggage at your destination. You can only take soft items into the plane with you, such as a small case which fits under the seat; nothing is put overhead.

One advantage of traveling by airplane is that those in the uniform of the airline are never tipped. Porters in the airport are tipped on the same scale as those in railroad stations.

STUDENT AND EXCURSION RATES

Many of the airlines today offer special rates to those between twelve and twenty-two if they are willing to fly on a standby basis. In order to qualify they must have a special youth card of identification which can be bought for a small fee at an airline office. This is good from the time purchased until the person is twenty-two, and is accepted by almost every airline. There are some times during the year when this offer is not valid, so a young person should check this with the airline.

The excursion plan, by which a person flies coach class at times and conditions specified by the airlines, cuts the cost of air travel by one-third.

Naturally passengers obey all signs that flash on during the flight and all orders from the stewardess or pilot.

SHIP TRAVEL

If one plans to travel by ship, reservations must

usually be made months in advance, and it's wise to book for the return trip at the same time. This is especially true for those traveling in the busiest tourist season.

PASSPORT, VISA, HEALTH FORMS

You must have a passport to travel to a foreign country. This is obtained by applying at a United States passport agency in person with a birth certificate, naturalization papers if you were not born in this country, some kind of identification and two passport pictures. There are specific requirements for these, so be sure to tell the photographer that you want the picture for a passport.

You will also need to check the particular requirements of the countries you'll be visiting. Some require that those entering the country have a visa. For some you will need immunizations, and these you should have sufficiently in advance to recover from the effects before traveling. You must have a smallpox vaccination within the past three years in order to get back into this country and a doctor's certificate of proof.

ADVICE OF A TRAVEL AGENT

If you are planning a trip abroad, you should check with a travel agent who can give you any information you need. He knows which countries require a visa, and he has the proper application blanks to fill out to get it. He will give you advice about carrying money and much other valuable help.

CLOTHES FOR TRAVEL

Someone has suggested that if you plan to travel abroad for a month, you should pack for a weekend. This may be a little exaggerated, but it is a reminder not to take too many clothes. To avoid having an excess of luggage to bother with, the traveler should invest in clothes that are of wash and wear, wrinkle-resistant material and can serve double duty.

Most ships have three classes—first, second or cabin, and third or tourist. There is no real reason for traveling first class unless you have a lot of money and want to spend it. The main inconvenience in the second or third class if you are traveling alone is the possibility of having to share a cabin with a stranger. The food and service in both these classes is of good quality and the price of the ticket is considerably less.

TABLE RESERVATION ON A SHIP

The first thing to do after getting settled in your cabin is to see the dining room steward to reserve a table. He will ask whether you prefer a table alone and whether you want first or second sitting. Which you choose depends on how early or late you wish to eat. You generally remain with your table during the entire trip and behave as you would at any table and with any guests.

CHAIR RESERVATION

You will also want to see the deck steward about reserving a chair if you plan to sit on deck a great deal during the trip. These are rented, so you cannot just walk along and sit down in any empty chair, for someone has already paid for its use.

TIPPING ON SHIPBOARD

Tipping on shipboard is somewhat more compli-cated than elsewhere because so many people are involved who serve you to a greater or lesser degree. Usually you are safe if you allow 10 percent of your passage money to cover tips. If your ticket costs five hundred dollars, about fifty more will be needed for tips. The cabin steward and/or stewardess, the dining room steward and the deck steward are always tipped at a ratio of about $10-$7-$5 depending on the class you are traveling. Usually the money is given to each in an envelope at the end of the trip. There are others who require tipping also. Be careful that you do not offer a tip to a customs official; it might be looked on suspiciously as a bribe.

DRESS ON SHIPBOARD

Friendliness is the general spirit on board ship. Though you may never meet these people again, you are bound together for these days in a particularly isolated way. Clothing is generally informal and casual although one should dress properly in the dining room. On a luxury liner first-class passengers dress in evening clothes (dinner jacket for men, dinner dress for women) every night except the first and last. On other ships evening dress may be worn by first-class passengers if they wish, though it is not required. Cabin and tourist class passengers seldom wear even-ing dress.

BEHAVIOR ABROAD

Those who go abroad have particular manners to

observe. These are important not only from the standpoint of courtesy between individuals, but also because the American abroad represents his country and his fellow Americans as no official government representative can. He is not just an individual American tourist; he *is* America, rightly or wrongly. The "ugly American" image is as much the result of thoughtlessness and unintentional rudeness as it is brazen disregard for the feelings of others. The American tourist should try to make friends for his country by not acting as though "we only are the people," but by appreciating the customs and the heritage of other countries.

LEARNING SOME FOREIGN WORDS

One of the best ways of doing this is to become familiar with the history, the customs and, to some extent, the language of the countries you plan to visit. The visitor going abroad should learn, or have a book which gives, the phrases he will need for everyday use. He should be able to greet people; to ask for the bill; to say please and thank you and the equivalent of "You're welcome"; to ask directions; to say, "I'm sorry, I don't understand" and "How much does this cost?" and to know words of appreciation. Small courtesies are sometimes better repaid by words of appreciation spoken in the language of the country than by a tip. The all too typical attitude, "I speak only English and expect you to do so also," is infuriating even in those countries where English is learned in school and can be spoken fluently.

DON'TS FOR THE TOURIST

The list of don'ts for the American traveler is long. Don't expect the same type of hotel service as at home unless you are staying in an American run hotel; don't demand a daily shower or bath; don't be loud and ostentatious in dress, behavior and equipment; don't expect to buy something for nothing just because it is "foreign"; don't act as though other people's money were play money; don't constantly compare unfavorably the country being visited with America; don't take pictures of·people and homes without asking permission and don't exclaim over how quaint they are; don't be niggardly about tipping, but on the other hand don't overtip; don't assume you may wear anything you want, and this means men in shorts with shirttails flapping loosely, and women looking equally sloppy.

In addition to the usual courtesies one would practice anywhere, some countries have their own specific customs to be observed. The traveler will be wise to check these with a travel agent and find out what is expected of him abroad. He will have a happier time and at the same time be an ambassador of goodwill for his country.

THE CHRISTIAN AN AMBASSADOR

Actually the Christian is just that wherever he goes —an ambassador for Christ. Paul put it so clearly: "We are ambassadors for Christ, as though God did beseech you by us: we pray you in Christ's stead, be ye reconciled to God" (II Corinthians 5:20). What further incentive for correct etiquette does the Christian need than to let his life be the kind that God can use to bring others to Himself?

INDEX